Strategies

That Promote

Student

Engagement

Second Edition

Unleashing the Desire to Learn

Ernestine G. Riggs
Cheryl R. Gholar

Foreword by Raymond F. Morgan

CORWIN PRESS

A SAGE Company

For information:

Corwin Press, Inc.
A SAGE Company
2455 Teller Road
Thousand Oaks, California 91320
E-mail: order@corwinpress.com

SAGE Ltd.
6 Bonhill Street
London EC2A 4PU
United Kingdom

SAGE India Pvt. Ltd.
B 1/I 1 Mohan Cooperative
    Industrial Area
Mathura Road, New Delhi 110 044
India

SAGE Asia-Pacific Pte. Ltd.
33 Pekin Street #02-01
Far East Square
Singapore 048763

Printed in the United States of America

Library of Congress Cataloging-in-Publication Data

Riggs, Ernestine Gates, 1938-
  Strategies that promote student engagement : unleashing the desire to learn / Ernestine G. Riggs, Cheryl R. Gholar. — 2nd ed.
      p. cm.
  Revised ed. of: Connecting with students' will to succeed : the power of conation / Cheryl Gholar & Ernestine Riggs.
  Includes bibliographical references and index.
  ISBN 978-1-4129-6318-3 (cloth : acid-free paper) —
  ISBN 978-1-4129-6319-0 (pbk. : acid-free paper)
  1. Motivation in education. 2. Teacher-student relationships. I. Gholar, Cheryl Renee. II. Gholar, Cheryl Renee. Connecting with students' will to succeed. III. Title.
  LB1065.G47 2009
  370.15′4—dc22

2008008420

This book is printed on acid-free paper.

08 09 10 11 10 9 8 7 6 5 4 3 2 1

Acquisitions Editor:	Cathy Hernandez
Associate Editor:	Megan Bedell
Production Editor:	Appingo Publishing Services
Cover Designer:	Lisa Riley

This book is dedicated to the millions of unsung heroes, who day after day, year after year, climb seemingly insurmountable mountains, swim against the currents of mediocrity, and race against the winds of defeat to provide emotional and physical support for any child in need. To those who go into battle, armed with love of the human adventure, knowledge of their craft, high expectations, and the belief that in spite of any adversity, they can and will make a difference in the lives of children. To those who fight real and imaginary dragons to open new ways of thinking, this book is dedicated.

To those who have an overwhelming commitment to the academic, emotional, and social development of all students, we honor the dedication of your work. To those who understand that the will to commit to the act of teaching moves one beyond intellectual somersaults that separate and divide schools of thought, placing little value on the worth of a child, we applaud you for having no time for "no-win verbal babble."

To those who are determined that the gift of knowledge will not slip through a child's grasp, we are humbled. To those who know that the act of teaching begins with faith in one's humanness, and resonates in the innermost lives of others, we are awe-inspired.

Authentic teaching and learning bring us to the deepest reality of our existence if, as teachers, we never lose sight of the human journey, and our ability to be moved by that which is important in life, including something as simple as a child's need to dream. This becomes the first step to attaining knowledge that triumphs over darkness. Authenticity initiates our collective expedition to the domain of conation and authentic success.

This book celebrates the facilitators of learning who know and actualize, on a daily basis, what it means . . . to teach.

Contents

Foreword

Raymond F. Morgan

Since the establishment of formal education, one of the most challenging tasks for educators has been opening a world of learning to students that moves them to reject the status quo notion of being in class, present yet absent, to choosing to actively learn as a participant and partner fully engaged in the process.

Most educators have talked about learning in terms of how cognition influences and shapes this process. Only a few educators in the last one hundred and twenty years have been examining and addressing the existence and significance of other factors that impact this age-old dilemma of having students understand and "buy into" the belief that they possess the power and capability within themselves to accomplish their dreams and aspirations. In other words, in addition to the cognitive domain, there exists the conative domain, or conation, which simply means the *will,* drive, and determination to achieve a goal and not give up until one's goal in school and/or life has been accomplished.

The concept of the *will* and its impact on our daily lives is not new, however not always fully understood. How often do we hear or read of some unbelievable feat performed by an ordinary person, who states that he or she was able to accomplish this because of "sheer will," or a seemingly terminally ill person lives beyond the predicated time of death by doctors, and states it is their "will to live" that prolongs their life? As previously stated, only a few educators have taken the bold step of elevating and transferring the importance and impact of the *will* as it relates to learning, thereby integrating conation with cognition. When experienced as an integral part of the same whole by learners, the two support each other, leading to greater understanding in the learning process and higher performance. Probably the first to understand the principles of conation and cognition was Emerson E. White. In his 1886 text, *The Elements of Pedagogy,* he wrote:

> It seems important to note in this connection that the development of the intellectual faculties is conditioned upon the corresponding development of the sensibility and the *will.* The activity of the mind in knowing depends, among other things, on the acuteness and energy of the senses, the intensity of the emotions and desires, and the energy and constancy of the *will.* (p. 92)

This wonderful quote spoke to the conative domain long before the term "conation" came into being. It gets at the heart of why an educational book should be dedicated to the conative domain in general and the concept of conation in particular.

Conation focuses on individual ***will*** and ***desire*** to succeed coupled with determination to not give up until success is achieved. White eloquently expresses how knowing is inexorably connected to an act of *will* on the part of the learner. He was not alone in this premise; years later, in 1917, Thorndike, in an article titled "Reading and Reasoning" in the *Journal of Educational Psychology,* theorized that comprehension and understanding had to take place under the proper influences, purposes, and demands of the *will.* In the middle of the 20th century, Mortimer Adler wrote of the negative aspects of children who can learn, but won't. In 1970, Emerald Dechant concluded in his text, *Improving the Teaching of Reading,* that the most important aspect of learning was what the learner was interested in, and what would enhance the learner's sense of self worth. In 1986, William Glasser, in his book, *Control Theory in the Classroom,* spoke of the importance of the conative domain (although he did not use the term "conative") in regard to children caring about learning and their own achievement. Despite all of the compelling statements over many decades from educators and researchers such as these about the importance of the will, very little quality research has been conducted concerning the conative domain and learning, especially in the area of the influence of *desire* and *will* and their effect on general achievement regarding learning, and with achievement specific to reading, given the current emphasis on high stakes testing.

There has certainly not, to my knowledge, been an entire book exclusively dedicated to the concept of conation. I should say there *was* not such a book until Ernestine Riggs and Cheryl Gholar came along with their pioneering effort in this uncharted area of study. Their text, *Strategies That Promote Student Engagement: Unleashing the Desire to Learn, Second Edition,* takes an in-depth look at how and why the will and desire to learn and succeed is manifested in some students and mysteriously does not surface in others. These authors clearly demonstrate, through creative, engaging, and intellectually challenging instructional activities, what conation means, how it impacts and enhances the cognitive domain, and why and how it is the underpinning of all aspects of learning, specifically in the core content areas. Using research-based strategies, they demonstrate possible solutions to helping underserved students with low expectations of themselves discover their individual and personal gifts, skills, and talents, thus increasing their self-esteem and self-efficacy.

This book is a real gem. It covers the topic of conation so thoroughly, taking on such tough subjects as courage in learning, character education, the end justifying the means, the conative character map, and the origins of success and failure. Especially useful is the Gholar and Riggs' Conative Taxonomy. My coauthors and I think their conative taxonomy is such a "cutting edge" paradigm that we present it in our textbook on content area reading. And now this book keeps getting better, as the new second edition promises to be chock-full of no-nonsense, but effective strategies for use in working with hard-to-reach children. As earlier stated, Riggs and Gholar are pioneers in the area of conation and reading and I can promise, you are in for a thoughtful exploration of exciting concepts and strategies which, when applied, can transform hesitant learners into students who hopefully will choose to surmount challenges along the road to learning. Through their eyes, you learn how the power of conation brings out the best in us as teachers and produces "take charge learners." Through conation, teachers and students can reimagine achievement and excellence!

Preface

Nothing can withstand the power of the human will if it is willing to stake its very existence to the extent of its purpose.

—Benjamin Disraeli

Sometimes in the quieting of our lives we free the power within us to work on matters of living deeply and learning fully every day. In order to give our best, we seek to know more of who we truly are and what we are becoming as professionals. Ask yourself: What does my best self as a professional and my best work really look like?

Once in a great while an idea comes along that really challenges us to change the way we think about teaching and learning. In this book you will examine the power of conation, the learning domain that moves student engagement into action. You will discover what's beneath instructional strategies that promote high performance. You will understand why students disengage from learning as you examine current and historical research, explore practical insights, read stories, and implement authentic classroom lessons and engaging instructional activities. You will examine the exceptional gift that resides within you in the conative domain. It will become clear why the "power of conation" is critical to initiating and sustaining student achievement. A unique view of hidden human capacity is provided.

This book is about *conation* or the *will*. Pronounced (koh NAY shun), it is a derivative of the Latin word *conatus*, which is defined as a natural tendency, impulse, or striving. Used in Spinozism philosophy, it is referred to as the inclination of a thing to persist in its own being. In Webster's *Third New International Unabridged Dictionary*, conation is defined as the conscious drive to perform apparently volitional acts, with or without knowledge of the origin of the drive, distinguished from affection and cognition. Good's *Dictionary of Education* defines the conative domain as "striving or having the power to strive or struggle toward a goal which may be conscious or unconscious; descriptive of one of the three great divisions of the mind or soul (historically), namely, the *will*, as contrasted with terms descriptive of the feeling (affective) or the power of knowing (cognitive)."

As Richardson, Morgan, and Fleener (2006) state in their textbook that focuses on reading in the content areas, "Even though this term has been used for almost 200 years in psychological literature, it is fairly obscure." Conation is known as "one of the rarest words in the English language."

Conation is the internal drive that pushes one beyond ordinary expectations and accomplishments. Conation is the heroic journey, the energy that says "yes" to new possibilities; the inner "toil," the inner work that sets us free. The *will* cultivates the power of belief by teachers, students, and parents that dreams are attainable and the impossible is possible. Students move in the direction of becoming positive and self-directed about life, education, and future goals; it is the inner will that transforms learning and, thus, living a life that is full and meaningful.

Growing research indicates that the dimension of its strength lies in an intangible place *within* the learner. Lepper (1988) defines *intrinsic motivated learning* as "learning that occurs in a situation in which the most narrowly defined activity from which the learning occurs would be done without any external reward or punishment." The act of learning and achieving become their own reward. This self-motivation, self-effort, striving, and volition are also referred to as conation.

What students believe about themselves, others, school, and the future shows up with them in school every day. Understanding the integral role of conation in academic achievement demystifies why some students choose to engage in learning and others choose to resist active participation. Encouraging and capturing the *will* to learn is critical to the learning process. The *will* to learn is the foundation upon which learning takes place.

Understanding the cognitive, affective, and conative domains and the interdependent roles they play in increasing academic and emotional strengths among students is critical to improving student outcomes. Books such as *Managing Your Classroom with Heart* (Ridnouer, 2006); *Activating the Desire to Learn* (Ssullo, 2007); *Stirring the Head, Heart, and Soul* (Erickson, 2001); and of course, the first edition of this book, *Connecting with Students' Will to Succeed: The Power of Conation* (Gholar & Riggs, 2004) all point to America's *educational* "wake-up" call as it relates to teaching with all domains in mind—cognitive, affective, and conative. The cognitive domain alone is no longer sufficient if we want to produce well-balanced future citizens. Even books written specifically for pre-service and practicing teachers, such as *Reading To Learn In the Content Areas* (Richardson & Associates, 2006), include conation, referencing *Connecting with Students' Will to Succeed: The Power of Conation* in one of its chapters. Throughout this content-area text, the focus is on the three domains that are crucial to struggling students overcoming social, psychological, and emotion barriers that interfere with learning.

Leading educational journals such as *The Middle School Journal, Journal of Adolescent & Adult Literacy, The Journal of Early Adolescent*, and *Educational Leadership* have featured articles on this topic. *Educational Leadership's* May 2007 cover was, "Educating the WHOLE CHILD." The article included a quote by Pablo Casals that stated:

What we teach children in school is 2 + 2 = 4 and Paris is the capital of France. What we should be teaching them is what they are: We should be saying: "Do you know what you are? You are a marvel. You are unique."

The conative connection focuses on two behavioral objectives:

1. *Knowing* what one has to do to achieve a specific goal

2. *Doing* what one has to do, intentionally giving one's personal best to achieve a specific goal

Empowered by applying the innovative knowledge embedded in conation, teachers can help students implement success strategies to jump-start and sustain learning over time. *Strategies That Promote Student Engagement: Unleashing the Desire to Learn, Second Edition* is unique in its approach, examining both the internal structure of learning and innovative strategies that teachers implement to help students bring out the best in their behavior, develop exemplary character, and achieve academic success.

This book is a celebration of learning and what happens when we focus on excelling. To excel demands exceptional attention to how to think, how to learn, how to stretch, and how to grow. It takes us on a journey to the places where learning lives and introduces readers to the concept of conative intelligence. Encouraging and capturing the will to learn is critical to the learning process. The will to learn is the foundation upon which learning takes place.

The fundamental underpinning of conation is goal-oriented action—action that leads to academic achievement. As we build character into the curriculum, along with academic standards, the conative domain provides a continuum of competencies. In the conative continuum we find goal-oriented action guided by ethical principles. We refer to ethical action in the conative domain as metaconation™. The strength of goal-oriented action is in direct alignment with student beliefs about themselves and the world around them. Conation, when released, is freedom—freedom to learn; freedom to change; freedom to grow; freedom to make wise, informed, and appropriate decisions; freedom to acknowledge and celebrate personal contributions, small and large.

You, as the guide on this journey, will teach students how to capture their vision, and run with their dreams. You will assist them in experiencing learning and life at higher levels of knowing and accomplishing. They will see the world through a new paradigm and themselves as students with energy, determination, and hope.

You will also benefit as you accompany your students on this journey. Parker J. Palmer (1998), in his book, *The Courage to Teach*, states: "To educate is to guide students on an inner journey toward more truthful ways of seeing and being in the world. How can schools perform their mission without encouraging the guides to scout out that inner terrain?"

This book is about the courage to not only "scout out the terrain" of learning, but to explore it in depth. It visits the concept of courage and what happens when one embraces tenets of change. As students read and learn about real people and/or fictional characters via the various instructional activities, they will be inspired by the tenacity, determination, and sheer *will* exhibited by these characters. Courage can look quite simple, but what goes on underneath the face of courage tells the story of who we are, how we move with the ebbs and flow of life during moments of joy and challenges or we retreat from it in times of darkness. Through stories and engaging activities, inspired by beliefs, perceptions of reality, and life itself, we see ourselves. As one well-known dreamer stated, "All our dreams can come true, if we have courage to pursue them." (Walt Disney).

They will stretch their thinking. The journey that is set forth is one of personal discovery, allowing many, for the first time perhaps, to unearth the value of who they are and what they are capable of. It is a journey that encourages students to celebrate their gifts and talents, and to view themselves beyond perceived limitations. They will learn what it takes to sustain attempts to climb mountains in their lives.

Conation captures energy, insulates pain, and inspires a passion for learning. In this unique domain we learn why energy continues to flow even in adverse conditions. Sadly, conation eludes those who choose not to know the power of who they truly are.

How does it work? Conation connects one to dreams; and dreams to the *will.* The *will* becomes bonded to a personal commitment, and suddenly one finds the inner self-working, often unstoppable toward a desired goal. Through the passion of the *will,* one pursues excellence; in the pursuit of excellence, one shortens the distance between the dream and reality.

Throughout the pages of this book you will gain insight, through theory and practice, focusing on the power of conation. You will find compelling references of how conation facilitates productive change even in the midst of distractions. You will learn how to put into practice strategies to help students move forward with their goals and yours. Instructional activities, stories, graphic organizers, questions, answers, reflection, rubrics, and more can be found throughout the chapters as you explore ways to promote high performance within your school community.

In the development of each chapter, thoughtful and reflective consideration is given to determine the content, organization, and format. In addition, current research has been included focusing on various educational principles such as learner-centered approaches, differentiated instruction, the impact of motivational factors on effective teaching and learning, productive teaching and learning environments, and cognitive, affective, psychological, and conative constructs. The instructional activities have been developed for primary through high school students and based on state and national standards.

Each chapter begins with a student and a teacher voice, acquired from elementary to high school students and from pre-service and practicing teachers who share their thoughts, feelings, beliefs, and philosophies on school, learning, teaching, and life. Research-based explanations and information about conation are explained in practical terms and through the implementation and application of authentic and engaging hands-on "Lessons from the Heart of Learning"

Instructional Strategies that are grade-level appropriate, performance-based, integrated with other content areas, provide for extended research opportunities, and utilize formal and informal assessments. The titles of each chapter indicate the focus and direction:

Chapter 1: Understanding Conation: Provides a historical background, research-based context, definition, and explanation of conation.

Chapter 2: Captivate, Connect, and Cultivate: Creating Lessons That Promote Learning: Provides a "walk through" of the organization of the "Lessons from the Heart of Learning." Teachers are provided with strategies that address the instructional needs of struggling and "low yield" students.

Chapter 3: Where Learning Lives: Instructional Strategies That Engage Students: Focuses on teaching and learning in the conative domain, through the engagement of students via authentic, standards-based instructional activities.

Chapter 4: An Invitation to Learn: Awakening and Motivating Your Classroom: Takes the reader on a heroic journey in pursuit of discovering how the "will" inspires dynamic and courageous teaching, awakening transformational and intrinsically motivated learning.

Chapter 5: For All of Them, I Teach: Reflecting on Your Teaching Philosophy: Teachers are challenged to reflect on and examine their personal teaching philosophies and their beliefs about and expectations of the students they encounter on a daily basis.

Chapter 6: The Bridge Between the Desire to Achieve and Reality Is . . . The Will: Putting It All Together asks you to reflect on the concepts of conation and metaconation in terms of your belief system and expectations of yourself and your students. Reflect on whether or not your paradigm has changed; if not, has this work given you cause to rethink some of your teaching practices?

HOW WILL YOU BENEFIT?

As a K–12 educator, you will learn effective tools to:

- Create an inspirational classroom environment
- Utilize effective models of differentiated instruction
- Examine the three domains of holistic teaching—cognitive, affective, and conative
- Broaden effective literacy skills and strategies
- Refine strategies for creating an inclusive classroom
- Develop comprehensive assessment techniques
- Maximize reading, writing, and thinking techniques across content areas
- Learn dynamic literacy and critical thinking skills strategies
- Teach to multiple intelligences in the classroom
- Move forward with fewer distractions
- Model standards you desire to see in others

- Invite peace into your leadership
- Release self-defeating thoughts
- Learn ways to incorporate personal gifts into your work

The dynamics of holistic teaching and learning evolve exponentially when levels of high academic performance and human development are elevated together.

If you are ready to be inspired, *Strategies That Promote Student Engagement: Unleashing the Desire to Learn, Second Edition*, is a must read. You are the most influential presence in the classroom. Students listen to your life as well as your lesson plans. As your educational life speaks with integrity and practical wisdom, you nurture academic success and emotional wellness. Conation, when utilized, is one of the most significant contributing factors to high performance, resilience, goal attainment, and personal achievement. This book will help you help your students connect with the power of conation and the will to succeed.

Integrity without knowledge is weak and useless, and knowledge without integrity is dangerous and dreadful.

—Samuel Johnson

Acknowledgments

First, we thank Corwin Press for recognizing the importance of this work and the value of its contribution to education. Their courageous stance is to be commended. We are truly indebted to Stephanie Jackson-Prather and Chris Jaeggi for taking the initial risk three years ago of buying into our belief that the concept of conation can help to make a difference in the lives of our young people.

We are sincerely grateful to our editor, Megan Bedell, for her insight, ideas, tenacity, thoughtful guidance, and enthusiastic "Sounds great" and "I am looking forward to this!" You are indeed a "cheerleader" and encourager.

We are intellectually grateful for current and historical research that validates our hypothesis and findings regarding conation as one critical link of momentous proportion to high performance. We acknowledge all who explore opportunities to transform ordinary classrooms into powerful places of learning. We honor all who demonstrate the academic courage to grow beyond their own, and perhaps others', expectations.

We are also exceedingly grateful to those courageous teachers who added to the authenticity of this book through their personal voices and those of their students. We thank Regina Alexander, Juwana Foster, Rhonda Kimbrough, Monica McClinton-Palmer, Sheryl Myrieckes, Jeannie Pimental, Lynn Rule, and Samantha Sims. We acknowledge the creative skills of Mitch Bejeck, for his years of visually crafting our ideas into colorful and engaging works of art that assisted us in effectively making our presentations meaningful for teachers, parents, and administrators. And we are most appreciative to Susan Ciucci for her ongoing friendship and guidance and for allowing us to use her as our sounding board.

As individuals first, and authors second, we would be remiss not to pay homage to significant individuals in our personal lives who have been living examples and role models of an unadulterated conative spirit and to those who have been our incomparable cheerleaders and supporters.

I hold in great esteem my parents, Theodore and Geneva, who led gently while inspiring my life with their values of wisdom and truths, which have served me well as I have chosen to serve others as a teacher and counselor. In their awesome reverence of God, they encouraged me to never wait for the sun but to be a light whether alone or in the presence of others. When possible, become an effectual collaborator with those seeking to create a new day.

I acknowledge my children, Tiffany and Christopher, for their accomplishments and struggles to find place and purpose to share their voices in the world. I have learned so much from them—of the resilience and fragility of the human spirit. To my husband, John, whose faith in me has always been my inspiration as well as my reality check. His tireless support during this project has given me the will to confront my own obstacles and stand firmly in my beliefs.

To my sister, Moonyueen, whose inner work and inner light taught me the virtue of silence, quiet time, and space for growing, healing, and reinventing myself. To my brother, Nicholas, and his wife, Helen, whose humorous and serious views of life have given me the gift of living purposefully, to dance with the twists and turns in life and laugh out loud at myself and the world when things get too crazy. To my sister, Teanna, and her husband, Jim, for being there to guide, support, and share their shoulders during times of stress—boosting my ideology of what's possible.

—Cheryl R. Gholar

As an educator who loves learning and awakening the thirst for knowledge in the lives of others, my appreciation for such an awesome gift goes to two of the greatest teachers I will ever know, my parents, Rufus and Catherine, who taught me to love God first, then myself; whose love, perseverance, and belief in my abilities provided me with indelible memories and tools of life, thus equipping me with their principles and wisdom, which serve as a firm foundation on which I have constructed my way of life and my sense of self-determination in matters that make a difference.

I especially want to remember one of my dearest friends, Dr. Anna Lowe, who was a role model of the conative spirit in her long battle with cancer. She never gave up hope, never stopped smiling, and by her sheer will of positive thinking and hope, amazed everyone who knew her. I really miss you, my friend! To my loving and talented son, Arnold, Jr., who is the center of my life; my loving and devoted husband, Arnold, Sr. (may he rest in peace); my sister, Margaret Thompson, who has been there for me through the laughter and tears, you are an untiring angel walking on this earth; my two very special friends, Lillie Pooler, who stepped up like a true champion, to stand by my side as a supporting ally in a very difficult situation; and Beverly Doss, who is dear to my heart; and of course, Nina Gates, my sweet, sweet other mom.

I also want to honor three educators who truly love their profession, who toil and teach with and from their hearts with a passion rarely seen . . . Karen Love, who is amazing, was first my student, now a true friend; Nick Salerno, assistant superintendent, and Annette Wiederholt, "a teacher's teacher"—both devote their lives and talents to the fortunate students in El Monte, California. All of you are the brightest stars in my universe with your own special brand of the conative spirit. And to five other significant people in my life—Dr. Judy Stewart, who calls me her "bestest friend" (Judy, the feeling is mutual), Gwendolyn

Traylor, Ednarene Smith, Arvon Prentiss, Sr., and Rev. Dr. D. Darrell Griffin, who, when you hear his story, will realize that conation is much more than a word (Rev. Griffin, you are an inspiration). My eternal thanks to all you for your love, prayers, encouragement, support, friendship, and for just being you! Each of you is an irreplaceable gift in my life.

—Ernestine G. Riggs

PUBLISHER'S ACKNOWLEDGMENTS

Corwin Press gratefully acknowledges the contributions of the following individuals:

Todd Boucher, Eleventh- and Twelfth-Grade Social Studies Teacher
Biloxi High School, Biloxi, MS

Dottie Flanagan, Kindergarten Teacher
Oak Grove Elementary School, San Antonio, TX

Michael Middleton, Associate Professor of Education
University of New Hampshire, Durham, NH

Melissa Miller, Sixth-Grade Science Teacher and
Science Department Chair
Lynch Middle School, Farmington, AR

Paul Parkison, Assistant Professor of Teacher Education
University of Southern Indiana, Evansville, IN

Tara Stevens, Assistant Professor of Educational
    Psychology and Leadership
Texas Tech University, Lubbock, TX

Elizabeth Strehl, Eleventh-Grade English Teacher
Canyon Springs High School, North Las Vegas, NV

Jennifer Wong, Third-Grade Teacher
Edward Gideon School, Philadelphia, PA

About the Authors

**Ernestine G. Riggs,** PhD, is an Associate Professor at Loyola University Chicago, teaching undergraduate and graduate students in the areas of reading, writing, research, character education, classroom management, and critical thinking skills; she is also an Associate Director of the Professional Development Consortium in partnership with Dr. Cheryl R. Gholar. Dr. Riggs received her degree in Educational Leadership and Policy Studies from Loyola University Chicago. She has completed advanced course work in reading, administration, supervision, vocational and diversity training, and human relations. She has been involved in the field of education for more than 40 years and has a diverse background in teaching. She has taught Head Start, primary, intermediate, upper grades, special education, and high school students. She also served in the position of Director of the National Diffusion Network and as a Senior Program Consultant for the North Central Regional Educational Laboratory (NCREL). Prior to joining the NCREL staff in 1991, Dr. Riggs was an administrator with the Chicago Public Schools, where she assisted in the implementation of reading and language arts programs for more than 500 elementary schools, 410,000 students, and 23,684 teachers.

The majority of Dr. Riggs' career has been in the Chicago Public Schools; however, she spent six years teaching in Misawa, Japan, under the auspices of the United States Department of Defense Overseas Schools. In addition to her teaching duties there, she was intensely involved with professional development. She organized exchange programs between Japanese and American teachers where she coordinated, and conducted workshops and training sessions on reading methods and instructional materials, diversity training, and human relations.

She is coauthor of *Beyond Rhetoric and Rainbows: A Journey to the Place Where Learning Lives; Helping Middle and High School Readers: Teaching and Learning Strategies Across the Curriculum;* and several journal articles. She is also cofeatured in the video *Ensuring Success for "Low-Yield" Students: Building Lives and Molding Futures.* In the summer of 2007, Dr. Riggs was invited to present a précis of the research on conation, conducted by Dr. Gholar and her, at the prestigious Oxford Round Table in Oxford, England.

Dr. Riggs' philosophy is that every child has the innate ability to learn and succeed in school and life, but that school and society often extinguish the flame of this ability. It is her belief that with a great deal of love, nurturing, authentic instruction, understanding, and encouragement, the conative spirit, or the will and determination to strive to be and do one's best, can be rekindled. She is a strong advocate of teaching the whole child, addressing the student's social, emotional, cultural, and environmental factors. She fervently believes effective learning begins with a positive perception of one's self and the way in which a person views the world. Self-efficacy and a positive self-concept are two essential ingredients for cultivating independent and successful learners. Her message is: **Perceive every child as having the potential for greatness; provide all students with the opportunity to succeed**.

She states, "I stay close to the human side of education by constantly reminding myself that 'no one cares how much you know, until they know how much you care.' My PhD stands for **P**ositivism, **h**umanistic, **D**evotion to helping all students learn and succeed in life."

Dr. Riggs is a member of numerous professional organizations; and is a frequent presenter at local, district, national, and international conferences. She has received numerous citations and merit awards, but considers her most distinguished recognition as that of being selected as one of the Outstanding Elementary Teachers of America by the United States Department of Defense Overseas Schools in 1974.

Cheryl R. Gholar, PhD, is Associate Director of the Professional Development Consortium, and has more than 30 years of experience in the field of education in the areas of teaching, counseling, administration in public schools, postsecondary education, character education research and evaluation, and grant writing. She is skilled in best practice identification in character education. Dr. Gholar has served a broad range of public and private clients, including state and local education agencies, as well as foundations specializing in leadership development and character education.

She is the coauthor of *Beyond Rhetoric and Rainbows: A Journey to the Place Where Learning Lives; Giving Kids the Will to Win;* and *Connecting with Students Will to Succeed: The Power of Conation.* Her research in the areas of resiliency and conation are cofeatured in the educational video *Ensuring Success for "Low Yield" Students: Building Lives and Molding Futures.* She is author and coauthor of numerous articles and special publications. Her work has been published in the *Chicago Tribune, Vitae Scholasticae, Black Issues in Higher Education, The Journal of Staff Development, Careers With Character,* and more.

Dr. Gholar is recognized nationally for offering cutting-edge leadership seminars that speak to the heart, mind, and soul of what matters most in schools, in the workplace, and in personal life. With vision and clarity, her seminars capture the power of synergy, personal fulfillment, and authentic success. A dynamic leader in the field of human potential with an original voice, Dr. Gholar has helped thousands to reinvest in their priorities and embrace the wisdom and genius that resides within.

Awards include Educator of the Year, Phi Delta Kappa; Outstanding Service to the Profession of School Counseling; Kate Maremont Award; Those Who Excel; Oppenheimer Family Foundation Award and Outstanding Service Award, Chicago Public Schools, Department of Character Education. She is listed in Who's Who Among Women, Who's Who in The Midwest, and International Who's Who of Professionals.

Introduction

The following excerpt is from a teacher in an urban school district:

> Creating an environment that encourages risk-taking and positive attitudes toward one another, as well as with oneself, begins when the students enter the classroom on the first day of school. As my students create a classroom "bill of rights," they realize they are being empowered with the ability to control their own destiny. They will be making choices that will affect them as learners, friends, and most importantly, as individuals. This enhances their inner will to think positively about themselves. To reinforce this thought, we have our classroom motto, *"If I think I Can, I Can!"* which is said after the pledge and is displayed in the room as a banner.
>
> The students know I will not give up on them, and they cannot give up on themselves! I know we have succeeded when students encourage one another in the classroom by saying, *"You can do it!"* or *"If you think you can do it, you will!"* This wonderful encouragement demonstrates an intrinsic understanding of believing in oneself and having the *will* to try.

This is conation! This is just one method or strategy teachers can use to help their students first discover, then understand they have a *will* and the power and ability to reach deep down inside of themselves to unearth these elements to become successful in school and life.

A large body of research has been conducted, and is ongoing, regarding extrinsic and intrinsic motivation. There has been much discussion, not to mention controversy, as to which tactic has the most effective impact on the learning process.

Teachers are confronted, on a daily basis, with the exasperating question: "How can I motivate my struggling or *'low-yield'* students, my second language learners, and those with disabilities to even make an attempt to learn the essential basic skills and strategies that will equip them to be able to compete in this technological and global society? How do I get them to want to learn without the issuance of gift certificates, McDonalds' coupons, or the promises of pizza parties?"

Extrinsic motivation (external influence) is too frequently utilized to "encourage" students to learn. However, there is a growing body of research that demonstrates the power of intrinsic motivation or "one's *inner will, drive, determination, tenacity,* and *perseverance* to want to learn," known as *conation* (Huitt, 1999). The *will* is this intangible place *within* each person that internally drives or compels one *to want to learn* for the personal value and self-satisfaction of learning (Gholar & Riggs, 2004).

Conation creates change from within. This transformation has the potential of refocusing our paradigm regarding the impact and influence the *will* has in the process of teachers *teaching* and students *learning.* Recognizing the reciprocity inherent between actions and their outcomes, research, instructional activities, and resources compiled in this book are dedicated to encouraging educational leaders of practices and perspectives that will foster sustainable courage, renewal, and authentic success for both teachers and learners.

Concerned with the deepest potentials of humanity and approaches that impact and transform learning, an examination of these concepts and a wealth of ideas, tools, and strategies that reach into the heart of learning, the place where conation resides, are provided. Conation has the power to transform the human condition. In classrooms where there is an understanding of how the conative domain impacts self-efficacy, self-motivation, and successful learning, teachers are aware that a coevolution of beliefs, ownership, and actions can produce authentic learning.

Conation is the work that precedes our victories and the resilience to bounce back from defeat or prevent it from happening. Preparing us to start all over again when necessary, we persist, strive, and move against obstacles, creating new paths that others often follow. The inner catalytic push toward greatness is needed in every student, in every classroom. When emotional determination, and academic energy join together as one force and action occurs, we experience the power of conation.

Resulting from the inner process of connecting vision, mission, beliefs, and intended goals to one's best self, conation builds and reveals character, courage, discipline, and personal leadership. *Action* is the operative word in the conative domain. *Intentional* is the action we seek in student learning. *Achievement* is the goal. When we examine authentic school success closely, we see *intentional academic achievement.* On a deeper level, sustained action over time crystallizes our way of being, informing us of who we are, the power and potential we possess, and as a result, what we are becoming.

At its highest dimension, conation is transformed into what the authors refer to as metaconation. Metaconation defines actions that fulfill and satisfy one's need for purpose, peace, meaning, internal harmony, and ultimately, what really matters most in school and in life. *Intentional* is the action in metaconation. Achievement of personal harmony that seeks goodness through *ethical behavior* is the goal. When we examine meta-conation closely, we see more than *"intentional behavior,"* we see *intentional ethical behavior."*

In the conative domain, teachers and students are invited to reflect upon their actions, responding to questions that include: "What will we do with what we know, with what we believe, with how we feel about ourselves as educators and learners and what we are required to teach and learn?"

Learning has some properties analogous to the growth of the Japanese carp or koi fish. Seemingly its growth potential is limited or expanded by the environment it's placed in. When in a small fish bowl, it will grow only two to three inches. Put in a larger tank or a small pond, it could reach six to ten inches. In a larger pond, the koi gets to be about a foot and a half. But if the koi is placed in a small lake, it can grow up to three feet long. Its growth is proportional to the size of its environment. It works this way for people as well. We grow according to the size of our world. A responsive environment that deems all students to be adept and important, believes that everyone has worth and something to contribute regardless of talent, or seemingly the lack of, expands the learner's capacity to reach, to grow, to strive.

Our job, as facilitators of learning and guardians of the flame of knowledge, is to develop strategies and models of behavior that teach, touch, and support the academic lives of all students. Through instructing and coaching with conation in mind, students learn academic and social decision-making skills that create stability and productive change in the learning process. Teachers, as change agents, enable learners to begin or continue their journey to excellence: informed, prepared, open to success, and hopefully, inspired to pursue life and education with meaning and passion.

We boldly challenge teachers to honestly scrutinize, analyze, and reevaluate their paradigm about the purpose of teaching and learning. It encourages teachers to courageously create conative connectivity in relationship to students as learners and teaching that effectively responds to students' needs, gifts, and capabilities.

The choice is ours, to integrate the wisdom of conation into the language of learning and our lives.

When we choose not to teach with conation in mind, we are doing no more than simply tossing out information while observing who will catch it. Yet, in reality, without the will to learn, information often gets caught up in the winds of chatter and verbal babble disconnected from the actual learning process.

Ultimately, this book is meant to encourage and inspire effective, authentic teaching, learning, and success by exploring ways to connect the heart, mind, and *will* of all students and teachers to the mission and promise that each and every student is entitled to the uninhibited pursuit and attainment of learning, and literacy, for life.

Who Are We?

Each of us is a limited edition, special and unique in our ways. We brighten the universe for a planetary moment, enlightening the world with rare and precious gifts. Wrapped in brilliance—a splash of magnificent glory released in slow motion. We are passion lit from within, a living journey seeking and giving light.

Introductory Thought

I can make you rise or fall. I can work for you or against you. I can make you a success or a failure. I can control the way you feel and the way you act. I can make you laugh, work, love. I can make your heart sing with joy, excitement, elation. Or, I can make you wretched, dejected, morbid. I can make you sick—listless. I can be as a shackle, heavy, attached, burdensome. Or, I can be as the prism's hue, dancing bright, fleeting, lost forever unless captured by pen or purpose. I can be nurtured and grown to be great and beautiful—seen by the eyes of others through action in you. I can never be removed, only replaced. I am a thought. Why not get to know me better?

—Robert Conklin

1

Understanding Conation

How do I know I'm successful in my personal life? Well, there's an inner light that glows so bright, I can never see myself giving up. I can describe my thoughts in one word—happy!

—Fourth-grade student

Once mutual trust is established we move forward to explore exciting possibilities that often have not been tried in reading instruction. Teachers discover new ways to engage and challenge students to learn. Innovative ideas are always welcome. Our work together is most gratifying, especially when we see rewarding results! At our school, we are a team. Teachers share with each other insights and strategies that are making a difference. Student involvement and test scores are increasing. I guess you can say that staff cohesiveness and accountability is evolving in ways that we are proud of as a school community.

—Elementary school teacher

WHERE DOES THE WILL TO LIVE, LEARN, AND SUCCEED RESIDE?

Educators have learned that we cannot make students learn. The age-old adage, "You can lead a horse to water, but cannot make it drink," applies aptly to students. We can teach them, attempt to motivate them, but we cannot learn for them. Students must be proactive in order to learn. First, they must possess the *will* to learn; then, they must make an effort and apply their energies to learning tasks.

Teachers cannot *give* students the desire, drive, or will. No teacher, parent, or any other stakeholder has the power to make students learn. *Drive, will,* and *effort* must emanate from the learner. However, teachers can awaken and cultivate these elements through authentic and creative teaching. This is not an impossible expectation, as these factors have been a part of the students' psychological structure since birth. Unfortunately, these elements are often overlooked, underestimated, or misunderstood. Teachers have literally ignored the payoff of these elements as they struggle through each day, trying to coerce students into learning the required subject matter.

The Will to Succeed

Teach From the Heart

Effective, knowledgeable, and empathetic teachers teach from the heart! Teaching that comes from the heart connects with the mind and soul of the learner. Teachers should assume responsibility for creating excitement, enthusiasm, and the will to learn, succeed, and survive in those students who have given up the race long before approaching the starting line.

The concepts of *will, drive,* and *effort* have been ignored too long by too many students. Students often think that learning is not very important in the scheme of things, and, therefore, they see little reason to devote a great deal of time and effort to their learning. It has been noted that at the middle school level, teachers should emphasize mastery and improvement instead of relative ability and social comparison. However, observed and empirical data has demonstrated that teachers do the opposite. Teachers place more prominence on relative ability, competition, and social status and less emphasis on self-motivation, effort, self-improvement, and life-planning strategies. This focus results in a decline in students' ability to perform tasks, a drop in their self-esteem and self-confidence, and, of course, lower academic achievement (Anderman & Midgley, 1996).

We are all teachers. We are all learners, in a place called life, with a gift called time. We must keep in mind that students who sometimes choose not to learn still have the capacity to learn. It may take time for them to say "yes."

Growing research indicates that the will to learn lies *within* the learner. The consequences are profound. Does this inner place have a name? Is it intangible and immeasurable? Current research exploring the psychology of learning examines the determinants of learning and how these determinants relate to the learners' willingness to take the initiative and the responsibility for his or her own learning.

What moves us and then makes us move? It is *conation*—the will, inner strength, determination, and volitional force that drives change. Conation connects us to our dreams; it connects our dreams to our *will*. When the *will* commits itself, we suddenly find our inner self working toward a goal. Through the passion of the *will,* we pursue excellence, and in the pursuit of excellence, we can live our dreams.

WHAT IS CONATION?

The distinction between volition, intellect, and emotion has been observed throughout the ages by puzzled and mystified scholars. *Conation,* from the Latin word *conari,* means one's capacity to strive. German and Scottish scholars in the late eighteenth century described the mind as having three capabilities or faculties: cognition (knowing), affection (valuing people, things, or ideas), and conation (striving and directing one's energy toward a goal). The idea of conation was ignored during the nineteenth and much of the twentieth century, because social scientists became disinterested in things you couldn't see or count. And, who can see something as abstract as the human will?

Huitt (1999) indicates that one reason why research into conation lagged behind research into cognition and emotion is that conation is often intertwined with the cognitive and affective domains and is difficult to separate from them. He explains that both Wechsler's scales of intelligence (Walsh & Betz, 1990) and Goleman's (1995) construct of emotional intelligence include conative components.

Recent research acknowledges that conation is essential to the acquisition of learning. Conation is critical if an individual is to engage in self-direction and self-regulation (Huitt, 1999). Since conation represents the will to act or freedom of choice, it is an essential part of human behavior (Bandura, 1997). The fundamental attributes of conation are:

- belief,
- courage,
- energy,
- commitment,
- conviction, and
- change.

These six attributes describe the fundamental framework of conation and how the act of learning occurs. *Belief* gives us *courage.* Courage inspires our powerful *energy.* Energy sustains our *commitment* to our goal(s). (See Figure 1.1.) When we activate and combine the first four attributes—belief, courage, energy, and commitment—we strengthen our *conviction*. When we purposely act upon our convictions, we experience internal and external *change*.

When we engage these six attributes, the possibilities for learning and making a difference are endless. These qualities must be in place for the teacher and learner to undertake the rigorous journey into the intensity, challenge, and excitement of learning. They provide clarity as to how and why we choose to learn and behave in certain ways.

Figure 1.1   Attributes of Conation

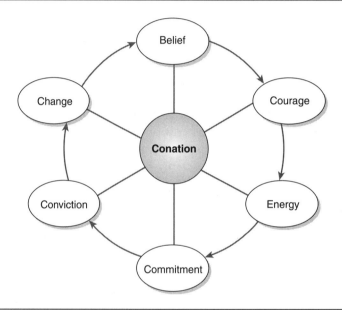

CONATION IN CONTEXT

As explained earlier, the mind historically has been divided into three parts—cognition (knowing), affection (feeling), and conation (will). The following paragraphs describe each of the three parts.

The Cognitive Domain

The cognitive domain, or cognition, can be defined as an intellectual process by which one acquires, stores, retrieves, transforms, and uses knowledge. An advanced form of cognition is metacognition. Metacognition occurs when learners are aware of their own cognitive processes and know when, where, and how to use these processes to facilitate and support their learning.

The Will to Succeed

The Gift of Conation

Conation releases you from fear of boundaries and limitations. It allows you to know instinctively that within you is a gift, the power to say "yes" to learning. Conation enables you to make choices in using your gifts to meet and exceed academic expectations.

Knowledge can be categorized into three basic elements:

1. **Content:** knowing what, where, and when (teaching skills)
2. **Context:** connecting knowledge with a task, environment, or expected outcome (researching skills)
3. **Cognition:** constructing knowledge through perception, reflection, critical thinking, and common sense (learning skills)

The learning process is multifaceted and complex, requiring the implementation of a variety of diverse teaching techniques. Researchers agree that there is no single approach—no made-to-order, foolproof *modus operandi*—that fully explains and demonstrates how children learn at the cognitive or metacognitive level. The behaviorists, cognitive psychologists, and social cognitive theorists all have their theories; each theory provides a piece of the puzzle, but none describes the ultimate solution.

Educators globally recognize Piaget's and Vygotsky's research and theories on how children construct knowledge. Piaget (1929) believed children constructed knowledge by assimilating and accommodating their physical and social environment. Vygotsky (1978) espoused that children acquire cognitive processes through guidance and interactions with others in their environs. He firmly believed that children were able to develop independently to a certain level, but had the potential, with the help and guidance of adults or peers, to advance to an even higher level of cognitive development. He called this the zone of proximal development (ZPD), which is the difference between what a child can do independently and what he or she can do with scaffolding or support. ZPD has become the underpinning for effective classroom instruction.

The Affective Domain

Affection can be defined as a feeling or emotion as distinguished from cognition, thought, or action. The affective domain addresses one's feelings, emotions, attitudes, self-perceptions, self-concepts, values, self-esteem, and self-efficacy. Research indicates that the affective domain significantly influences one's ability to learn or perform (Bandura, 1986).

The Will to Succeed

Sowing Seeds of Success

As teachers we must focus all of our energy on cultivating the seeds (our students) and preparing and tilling the soil (promoting learning that renews and transforms itself) if we hope to harvest beautiful, ripe fruit (students who are mentally, emotionally, socially, and intellectually healthy and productive). When teaching and learning are transparent and fluid, students discover that the possibilities of education and life are limitless, students believe in their potential to be the very best that they can be, and students realize that they can become a truly "no limit" person.

The affective domain also plays a pertinent partnership role in the confluence of conation. Both affection and conation are connected to motivation; affection is connected to extrinsic motivation and conation is connected to intrinsic motivation. Affection plays a role in learning: Students' positive or negative reactions and responses to learning goals and performance tasks are, unfortunately, often dependent upon their positive or negative relationships and interactions with peers, parents, and teachers.

Our dreams are only limited by how far our beliefs and actions will take us.

The Conative Domain

In *Flow: The Psychology of Optimal Experience* (1990), Csikszentmihalyi describes conation as intrinsic motivation, coming from within. Conation is the inner strength that compels us to reach down to the depth of our will in order to reach a goal or complete a task. This inner strength can be equated to self-actualization in Maslow's (1987) Hierarchy of Needs. However, some theorists explain that "students are most likely to be intrinsically motivated when two conditions exist:

1. they have high self-efficacy regarding their ability to succeed at classroom tasks, and
2. they have a sense of self-determination—a sense that they have some control over the course that their lives will take" (Ormond, 2000).

Figure 1.2 summarizes the facets of the cognitive, affective, conative, and metaconative domains and illustrates the differences and the interconnectedness between each domain.

Teachers can help students, as well as themselves, better understand the role conation plays in learning and how it operates in relationship to the cognitive and affective domains. These domains are interrelated when applied to the learning process, but are distinctly different in terms of the philosophical and instructional focus.

Figure 1.2   Comparing the Cognitive, Affective, Conative, and Metaconative Domains

Domain	Attributes	Examples
Cognitive	Knowledge, intellect, problem solving, critical thinking, reflective thinking, comprehending	I must learn at least three major causes of the Civil War and how these causes impacted the later events in US history.
Metacognitive	Awareness of cognitive processes and how to use them	I will create a cause-and-effect graphic organizer to help me remember the information.
Affective	Feelings, emotions, enthusiasm, self-perception, self-concept, values, beliefs	This is a great assignment but I feel uncertain about my knowledge of the topic and my research skills. As I work on this project, there are times that I feel extremely unsure of myself.
Conative	Will, perseverance, persistence, determination, patience, tenacity, self-efficacy, intentionality	I am really having a difficult time with this assignment, but I am determined to write one of the best essays ever created on this topic. Conation keeps us in touch with what we are capable of.
Metaconative	The ethical application of "knowing" to learning and life, action directed toward the highest good, action intended to achieve a virtuous goal, ethical, moral behavior; honesty, respect, courage, integrity, responsibility, caring, empathy, trustworthiness	I had the courage to continue studying and exploring the value of the project and the good that comes from knowing all aspects of the truth. Metaconation reminds us of the significance of our actions and the choices we make.

Although we have described the domains in linear order, with separate and distinct attributes, we do not intend to rank the domains according to their importance in the learning process, nor do we wish to give the impression that the domains are independent of each other. To the contrary, the cognitive, affective, and conative domains are very much interconnected and interdependent.

BELIEVING IS SEEING

When we see students as individuals charged with natural curiosity and filled with potential, we tend to provide them with opportunities to succeed, and we expect them to succeed. Consequently, students' will to succeed is engaged. This increases the likelihood that students learn the content and are imbued with the desire to continue to learn. On the other hand, if teachers communicate explicitly (with insensitive remarks) or implicitly (with closed body language or low expectations) that their students are hopeless or hapless, student success will be the exception rather than the rule. Our beliefs about who we are and who students are determine how we treat students and what and how we will or will not teach them. And these beliefs, unfortunately, will affect what students believe about themselves. Our beliefs are reflected in our actions. What we believe about students is what we see in them. A person's worldview is the paradigm through which they perceive reality.

Understanding that believing is seeing is essential to considering how success and failure are born and nurtured in the lives and minds of our students. *Success* begins with a belief. *Failure* begins with a belief. How students act upon specific beliefs informs us of how they see themselves, how they view school and the world around them. Our beliefs build our individual view of the world, creating our paradigm (see Figure 1.3).

INTENTIONAL ACTION

Intentional action—building upon the "winner within"—can be a powerful force in learning and can raise student performance in highly significant ways. According to Kolbe (1990), the "I will" factor is more important than IQ. Students have the power to accomplish amazing intellectual, social, ethical, and economic feats when they engage their conation. We all know stories from literature and real life of individuals who simply believed in themselves, worked toward specific goals, stayed focused, relentlessly persisted, challenged the status quo, and pushed themselves, and by so doing, created new ideas, methods, opportunities, technologies, medical breakthroughs, and social advances. The power of ordinary people to do extraordinary things for themselves and others is the nature of conation.

Figure 1.3   The Conative Paradigm

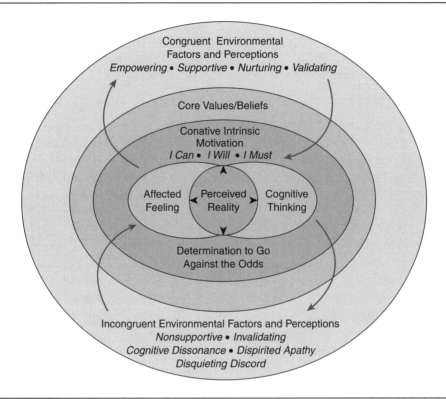

HOW IS CONATION DIFFERENT FROM EXTRINSIC MOTIVATION?

Extrinsic *(external)* motivation—Learning or the effort to learn takes place when an external incentive such as a prize or perhaps the avoidance of punishment is brought before the learner. While sharing my thoughts on the topic of extrinsic motivation, I was told the story of a young man who worked diligently in the fields of Georgia for months taking care of the family crops.

The fruit and vegetables that particular year were beautiful and in abundance. Excited about his bumper crop and how his hard work had paid off, he was proud that soon he would be able to take his harvest to the market in town. Overloaded with produce, his wagon could hold no more. So heavy was the produce, the old horse the family had was barely able to pull the wagon. The owner encouraged the horse to keep moving toward

In committed teacher-student learning communities, learners are engaged, not just put to work.

town. He placed carrots and apples in front of him and cubes of sugar. The carrots dangled in front of the horse's eyes, tempting him to stay on course. Being hungry, the horse's goal was to reach the carrots in order to satisfy his hunger. Assuming the horse would follow the carrots, the owner's extrinsic motivator, food, got the horse to pull the wagon to town.

Extrinsic and Intrinsic Motivation

Conation and intrinsic motivation share in part the same learning domain—the conative domain. Intrinsic motivation to learn is one's personal desire to learn without involving external rewards or undue pressure. Intrinsic motivation is personal inspiration (Ormrod, 2006). Conation is a personal call to action, i.e., Now that I am inspired, what will I do? It is the actual work that moves desire and inspiration into reality. It is the effort and the unstoppable will, drive, and determination to sustain goal-oriented action. I remember hearing an incredible story of a father who lifted a car by himself off of his child's leg in an effort to save the boy's life.

A law student shared with me a few years ago his compelling effort to stay in law school. He didn't do well his first semester and hoped his grades would get better the next semester. However, they didn't. He told me, "My first year of law school just didn't go right, there were too many distractions." Despite the poor grades that pushed him out of school, he met with the dean and posed an unusual question. He began by saying "I've wanted this opportunity all of my life. I'm not certain what happened." Not to be dissuaded from his goal, the student put forth his best effort and asked, "If I complete a year of school to become a paralegal with all As, can I meet with you this time next year about returning to law school?" The dean said, "Yes." The young man gave up his job and studied relentlessly, made all As, and completed a paralegal program. The dean kept his word. The student was readmitted and graduated among the top of his class.

We all know heroic stories of remarkable journeys that we have personally taken, journeys of challenge and triumph, pain and victory, losing and winning, falling and getting up. How do we move from failure to success? It begins with a belief, a personal belief that will not rest until we take action, a belief that defines what matters most in our lives. When the power of conation calls us to action, we find that within us there is so much more to give and receive. Ultimately, we find ourselves giving our all!

The power of conation makes the seemingly impossible, possible. We all have this power. Often unaware of it, it remains an untapped frontier. We can make use of its energy, drive, and determination or we can turn away from it. Conation shows up as a partner in teaching and learning when we show up to teach and learn.

Conation is the intrinsic preparation we must face in order to challenge the rigor of today's demanding curricula. Have you ever seen a person win an international marathon and never put forth any effort, never give it an initial thought, refuse to prepare for it, and have no interest? Internal preparation begins with one's desires, intentions, beliefs, and actions. Internal preparation sets the stage for the choices the learner will make—what the learner will try or refuse to try. When the desire to learn is greater than the choice not to learn, everything inside of the learner actively prepares for the learning process to begin. The learner gives the task at hand his or her all. The results are the best the learner can give at a specific time. The results can also be seen as change in behavior, cognitive, affective, and conative. Conation is the inner toil or inner work that sets us free to become who we truly are. Exciting performance gains can be achieved through student engagement. Therefore, it's time to put the "carrots" away and start igniting fires!

WHAT IS CONATIVE INTELLIGENCE (CI)?

Conative intelligence (CI) is the ability to persist, pursue, strive, and commit to a goal; understand the role of persistence in high performance; and productively engage the energy of the will in active teaching and learning. Effective learning communities seek to generate and sustain excellence. Conative intelligence embraces the will to succeed in all aspects of education and life. When people engage their conative intelligence, they strive to make wise, self-directed, cognitive, and affective choices. They also nurture, support, and energize their inner will to pursue personal and academic goals (Gholar & Riggs, 2004).

Core Components of Conative Intelligence

The nine components of conative intelligence demonstrate qualities inherent in successful students and teachers. Persons who display conative intelligence have willingness to

- believe,
- understand,
- hope,
- strive,
- give,
- give up ineffective paradigms,
- focus,
- change, and
- pay exceptional attention to their own intentions.

Conative intelligence builds resilience. Resilient teachers and students demonstrate

- flexibility,
- optimism,
- endurance, and
- an openness to learn.

Resiliency is a personal trait of every successful leader and learner. Individuals who are resilient accept change more readily and recover more quickly from adverse situations, misfortune, and hardship. They live in the present but find comfort in looking toward the future. Conative intelligence increases our ability to capture and hold on to success through belief, energy, courage, conviction, and change (see Figure 1.4).

Figure 1.4   Using the Power of Conation

Belief	Stepping into the world of the will (conation)
Courage	Choosing to grow by finding personal meaning
Energy	Discovering your personal worth inside of you
Commitment	Changing as needed in order to learn, live, and become your personal best
Conviction	Inspiring others to learn and find themselves by your actions, choices, and expectations
Change	Transforming knowledge into wisdom

What does conation really look like when applied to one's life in the real world? Read the true stories of Ki and Angie. Review the elements in Figure 1.4 again, and you will see the impact conation has on individuals, much like you, who have discovered their power within.

Ki's Story

Ki is a Native American, born on a reservation. She spent her formative years in this environment, attending elementary, middle, and high school. Unfortunately, many of her peers did not make it through middle school, and many more never graduated. A number of those who did graduate and ventured out into the "other world," out of their familiar surroundings, away from loving and supportive friends and family, returned to this safe haven because they were not prepared to face the demands of the society outside on their own.

However, Ki was different. She not only graduated from high school, but also went away to college, earned a BA, and a Masters degree. Ki is now back home, by choice, to teach and be a role model for other Native Americans, both children and adults. When asked how she broke this cycle of defeat and failure that so many of her friends became victim to, she simply replied, "I was determined to do something with my life! I knew I wanted to be a teacher, and be a teacher here at home. It was scary and kind of difficult at first, trying to fit in, learn new ways and yes, even a new language (slang); but I knew I had to be successful, for my mother, my father, but most of all for me. So I got to the university and stuck with it! Now I am back home, with my first teaching job, and proving to my students that it can be done."

Angie's Story

Angie, a senior in a large urban high school, was a quiet, serious student who made average grades, but seemed to work extremely hard. She really cared about school. She would always get information missed regarding assignments, but her constant tardiness annoyed her teacher tremendously. When asked about her habitual tardiness, and scolded about being irresponsible, Angie would not respond. Finally, after a month of this, the teacher became furious and thought of barring her from class for a week, just to teach her a lesson, and demonstrate to the class who was in charge. If the other students could get to school on time, she just couldn't understand why Angie could not, and as Angie did not provide any excuses, she just perceived her as too lazy to get up on time.

One day, consulting a teacher who had Angie in class the previous semester, her current teacher was informed that Angie's mother died two years ago. As the story unfolded, being the oldest child at home, Angie was left with a set of preschool twin siblings, and a remorseful father to look after. Angie's father wanted her to drop out of school and care for the twins while he worked to support the family. His salary would not cover day care costs.

However, Angie wanted to stay in school and graduate, but could only do this if she found someone to take care of her siblings. With the help of the school counselor, a day care center run by a church was found and it was free. The only problem was the location. She had to travel several miles to get there each morning before going to school. Her father told her that if she could get the twins there and pick them up in the evening, she could stay in school. Angie had to take two busses in order to reach the day care center, then take two buses back to her school, and repeat the route after school.

She had been going through this routine since her junior year. When asked by her teacher why she never explained this to her, Angie replied that it wasn't a big deal. It was just something she had to do if she wanted to graduate and graduating was very important to her because she had to go to college to fulfill her dream of becoming an accountant. She knew what she wanted and knew what it was going to take to reach her goal. So, she did what she had to do.

Stretching the boundaries of possibilities involves shattering old conventions. Energies devoted to finding new ways to address issues in education opens opportunities for touching the heart of learning, namely, issues facing the human side of the curriculum. One's beliefs and perception of reality can impact the outcomes of teaching and learning. It is important to keep in mind that shadows and transformations can be birthed into life, or become stillborn, due to a lack of nurturing on the human side of the curriculum. The human side of the curriculum drives the performance side. In helping students confront the reality of who they are, we enable them to explore the truth and fiction about what they can and cannot do with their lives.

Students with character walk not in your shadow but in your light.

When the world around us seems fragile, dysfunctional, or impoverished, our belief, energy, courage, commitment, conviction, and change systems can become our gravity. They pull us down, hold us back, and reduce our personal expectations. Overcoming the dynamics of gravity requires the force of powerful engines that lift our systems of engagement and strengthen our capacity for learning. When all systems are "go," learning takes flight and we know exactly where we are going. Conation is a call to action.

2

Captivate, Connect, and Cultivate

Creating Lessons That Promote Learning

Success doesn't always mean that you have to be at the top of the class. For me it means understanding what you have to do. When I understand the task that is before me, I do it. There are many times that I need help and I ask for it. My mom, my teacher, and my friends and I work together. They are not afraid to stop me if my work is incorrect. I ask a lot of questions and I try. I do my best to keep up. My grades are getting better. Always ask for help and you'll get it.

—Elementary student

Every child is capable of learning. If a teacher is not getting through to a child, then it is the teacher's responsibility to find a way to get the child to learn—make the light bulb go on.

—Elementary teacher

CONATIVE STRATEGIES FOR ENGAGING LEARNERS

Why is conation important to the learning process? Conation transforms ability into action—the process we use to fulfill our goals (Kolbe, 1990).

Motivation sets the stage for action and conation carries out the action (Corno & Kanfer, 1993). The conative domain connects to new adventures in learning. It provides a construct or model for teaching students new concepts (see Figure 2.1).

Figure 2.1   The Three C's of Connation

- **Captivate:** Seize students' attention with interesting, grade- and subject-appropriate materials and authentic tasks.

- **Cultivate:** Foster and encourage the development and refinement of students' abilities, skills, gifts, and talents.

- **Connect:** Establish a bridge between what is taught and what is learned.

—Adapted from Hixson, Gholar, & Riggs, 1999

This chapter provides a variety of strategies and activities based on the concept of conation (the *will, determination,* and *internal drive* to succeed). These activities have been designed to empower students' sense of well-being and rekindle their hearts with a commitment to becoming the best they can be. The activities help students thoroughly examine their beliefs about who they are and about what they can achieve. The goal of each activity is to address a holistic approach to teaching and learning. The activities blend the conative, cognitive, and affective domains in an integrative and cohesive manner. The activities will help students become aware of their own conative abilities, improve their cognitive skills (literacy and critical thinking), and enhance their affective (emotional) development.

In the conative domain, the learner engages his or her action and will to produce academic persistence. The purposeful desire to strive and the determination to acquire knowledge or a skill are critical to student achievement and authentic success. Students with conation are ready to accomplish a task. If conation is infused into the synergy of learning, the result will be a self-motivated, competent, knowledgeable, and productive learner.

In the conative domain, a teacher's attempt to facilitate learning becomes actualized through the individual student's will, drive, and effort to achieve. Learning is transformed into the acquisition of knowledge. Conation sets in motion the charge to learn and the responsibility to carry out that charge. In moments of internal conflict, the charge to excel will overpower the temptation to procrastinate in completing the task at hand, or to ignore it altogether. Conation tackles every obstacle, carries the learner forward, and propels the student to achieve or surpass the intended goal. Conative learners take charge of their learning. Through persistence, the learner transforms potential into reality.

Teachers not only have the power to help students achieve their dreams, they can also help students discover their dreams. Teachers can encourage students to ascertain what gives them enjoyment, to find harmony in their lives and environment, to determine a sense of purpose, and to discover their own conative capacity (internal drive). If students own these ideas, they are better equipped to cope with life's challenges, disappointments, and other obstacles.

DESIGNING LESSONS THAT REACH THE HEART OF LEARNING

Research has indicated that students learn more effectively when they are more actively engaged in their own learning (Wolfe, 2001). Therefore, conative lessons must be active. Conative lessons must also be

- personally relevant,
- appropriate (to students' developmental level),
- authentic (intellectually intriguing),
- challenging yet safe (without fear or potential for embarrassment),
- collaborative,
- flexible (providing students a number of ways to demonstrate learning), and
- adaptable (offering appropriate options).

The lessons that appear at the end of every chapter are exemplars of conative instructional design.

Each lesson begins with a thoughtful and reflective quotation that can be used to engage the learner in a critical analysis of its meaning and how it relates to her or his life. Each lesson includes the following components with explanations.

What's It All About

- The name of the instructional activity accompanied by a quote.

- **Purpose:**
  Conative learning begins when the teacher and learners know why they are engaging in a particular activity and how the activity will improve their sense of conation. A minimum of three purposes are identified for each lesson. An example of a purpose is: "To promote one's understanding of his or her own ability to achieve a desired goal."

- **Instructional Objectives:**
  These statements describe observable behaviors and actions that students should be able to do by the end of the lesson. Remember to align these objectives with your state and district standards.

- **Interdisciplinary Implementation:**

  Research shows that learners benefit when learning standards from different content areas are combined within the same lesson or unit (Ellis & Fouts, 1997; Jensen, 2001; Shanahan & Newman, 1997). Providing interdisciplinary activities

  - increases the learners' motivation (will to learn),
  - assists learners in discovering and connecting concepts, and
  - helps teachers manage an overloaded curriculum.

- **Instructional Focus:**

  This section identifies the content that will be taught. We recommend using the life stories of real people. Examining the lives of other people helps students examine their own lives and find personal meaning in their learning.

Making the Connection

- **Instructional Strategies and Activities:**

  This section describes the step-by-step process used in each lesson. See Using Teaching Strategies Effectively in the Conative Domain for learning strategies you can use to develop this section of the lesson.

Conative Insight: Now That I *Know*, What Will I *Do*?

- **Extended Research and Reflection:**

  This section provides direction for further student research on the topic of the lesson. One way to know if a student has begun to work within the conative domain is if she or he exhibits a desire to learn more about a given topic. Students should be given opportunities to explore the lesson topic outside of the lesson plan.

  During the reflection stage of the lesson, students are given an opportunity to think more about what they have learned. Without metacognitive time, true learning cannot occur. Use open-ended questions to facilitate reflection.

Assessment

The Fifth Discipline Fieldbook asserts that "change and learning may not exactly be synonymous, but they are inextricably linked" (Senge et al., 1994). Any assessment plan should provide varied opportunities for students to exhibit how they have changed. Conation is about change. In addition, teachers should assess the power of their lessons to bring about change and refine their lessons to increase their effectiveness.

USING TEACHING STRATEGIES EFFECTIVELY IN THE CONATIVE DOMAIN

The strategies that follow are, for the most part, open-ended or non-prescriptive. Therefore, they provide students with opportunities to construct meaning and connect to their prior knowledge and experiences. When these strategies are constructively woven into lessons, students are able to make conative connections to the lesson topic and thereby enjoy a positive learning experience that will stay with them.

The Will to Succeed

A Wellspring of Learning

Deep within each person is the conative domain—the will, drive, and determination to succeed. We can tap into a wellspring of learning, the heart of the matter, the place where fortitude, commitment, adaptability, and persistence are nurtured, if we, as educators, have the will.

Anticipation Guides

Anticipation guides, as the name infers, help students make predictions. Anticipation guides usually include four to ten stereotypical or controversial statements. The statements are usually written in a yes-no, agree-disagree, or true-false format. Students read each statement and draw conclusions based on what they know, what they think they know, or what they can guess before they read a selection or learn about a new topic. After students complete the anticipation guide, they read the text or learn about the topic in order to determine how accurate their predictions were. Some sample anticipation guides are shown in Figure 2.2.

Anticipation guides are designed to motivate students to

- rely on their own metacognitive skills,
- evaluate the statements or issues based on their individual paradigms,
- access and use their prior knowledge to make sensible inferences, and
- debate the issues without the restrictions or limitations of having "the right answer."

Using an anticipation guide in the conative domain provides each student with the opportunity to experience cognitive, affective, and conative success. Some teachers are not aware of the fact that many students have never experienced the joy or sense of accomplishment in knowing what it feels like to "have that right answer" or have their opinion accepted and valued, regardless of how far out of the box it may seem.

Figure 2.2   Sample Anticipation Guides

Primary Example

Anticipation Guide for *How the Sea Became Salt*

Circle Yes if you think the answer is correct. Circle No if you think the answer is not correct.

Yes	No	1.	This story is about a sea who wanted to be salt.
Yes	No	2.	Everyone loves the taste of salt.
Yes	No	3.	Salt is good for you.
Yes	No	4.	This is a true story.

Intermediate/Middle School Example

Anticipation Guide for *The Witness (Ash-Shahid)*

If you agree with the statement, circle Agree. If you disagree with the statement, circle Disagree.

Agree	Disagree	1.	This story is about someone who is a witness to a crime.
Agree	Disagree	2.	Ash-Shahid is the witness.
Agree	Disagree	3.	Ash-Shahid is not an American.
Agree	Disagree	4.	This story is not about a crime.
Agree	Disagree	5.	People who are witnesses always tell the truth.
Agree	Disagree	6.	Someone who is a foreigner cannot be a witness.
Agree	Disagree	7.	Witnesses must swear to tell the truth or they go to jail.
Agree	Disagree	8.	Children cannot be a witness.

High School Example

Anticipation Guide for *The Topic of Graphs*

If you think the statement is correct, circle True. If you think the statement is incorrect, circle False.

True	False	1.	Everyone is smart in math.
True	False	2.	Graphs are charts that show comparisons.
True	False	3.	Graphs can always be used to help you understand a problem.
True	False	4.	Newspapers do not use graphs.
True	False	5.	Students should be required to make graphs for problems they don't understand.
True	False	6.	Only students who are good in art can make graphs.
True	False	7.	Students who know how to do math should not have to make graphs.
True	False	8.	Students in elementary school are not smart enough to understand graphs.
True	False	9.	Bar graphs are the easiest to make and understand.
True	False	10.	Students who cannot make good graphs are not smart.

Using anticipation guides is one way to captivate, connect, and cultivate students' will to want to learn and participate in the process of learning and doing. Why? Because the student has a fighting chance of succeeding, of demonstrating that he or she has something to offer, and proving that he or she has a brain. These guides give each student (as well as the teacher) an opportunity to explore and discover their multiple intelligences. When students realize the threat of failure has been diminished or eliminated, they are more willing to take risks. They exhale the fear of disappointment, embarrassment, and degradation, and inhale the feeling of self-worth, achievement, and even triumph.

How many teachers have experienced that awesome moment when Timothy or Samantha discovered where to find the "switch" (in their own mind, will, and brain) and turned on the light ("I got it!")? When students are given the opportunity to become intentional inquirers and self-discoverers and experience success in their pursuits, they will likely become willing participants in the learning process.

Graphic Organizers

Graphic organizers are visual representations. They are also referred to as:

- visual organizers
- semantic maps or webs
- structured overviews
- mind maps

Graphic organizers are mental tools that learners use to aid in their understanding and remembering. Research has indicated that a large percentage of students are visual learners. Therefore, graphic organizers are effective learning tools, because they include both visual images and words.

Research has proven that graphic organizers are one of the most effective instructional strategies in improving comprehension (Ogle, 2000). They are instructionally "universal"; that is, they can be used with any subject, content area, and grade level. They are also effective with all types of students—from the gifted to those with special needs (Lehman et al., 1992; Sorenson, 1991). They also promote vocabulary development (Toms-Bronowski, 1983).

There are many types of graphic organizers. Following is an explanation of two of the most frequently used graphic organizers and how they may be used to enhance instruction.

Semantic Webs

These graphic organizers help learners discover and create connections between ideas. Students are usually given a topic and are asked to brainstorm ideas connected to the given topic.

The semantic webs in Figure 2.3 show some brainstormed ideas about the causes of failure and the causes of success in school and in life. You may use the blackline master in Figure 2.4 to practice creating a semantic web. Use the blackline on your own or adapt it for use with your students.

Semantic Feature Analysis (SFA)

The semantic feature analysis (SFA) graphic organizer provides students with a visual technique to simply and effectively compare the characteristics of different ideas, objects, concepts, views, or beliefs. SFAs help students comprehend and learn required material. In turn, students gain an effective tool for overcoming instructional challenges and succeeding in learning required material. An example SFA is shown in Figure 2.5.

INCREASING STUDENT SELF-EFFICACY WITH CHOICE

Students must *choose* to learn. Choice is an important factor when designing instruction in the conative domain. Teachers can nurture student self-direction and personal efficacy by providing students with choices prior to, during, and after lessons. This doesn't mean that students will make all the decisions, nor does it mean reverting to personal relevance curricula of the 1960s. When we emphasize student self-direction and efficacy, we use strategies that offer students opportunities to make decisions and solve problems on their own. Students learn to process information with confidence, come to believe that they have the ability to strive to succeed, begin to set their own goals for personal development and instructional improvement, and plan how they might achieve their goals. Perhaps most important, students become more reflective about their thinking and what they are learning. "[W]hen students are working on goals they themselves have set, they are more motivated and efficient, and they achieve more than they do when working on goals that have been set by the teacher." (Hom & Murphy, 1983)

From the business world, we know that people who attain success are those who plan, identify goals, and design strategies to work toward those goals (Peters & Waterman, 1982). Likewise, students must learn a variety of problem-solving strategies in order to reach their goals. In order to solve complex problems, students should learn to talk through the problem, and

- ask what they know and what they need to find out,
- pose questions,

Figure 2.3   Sample Semantic Webs

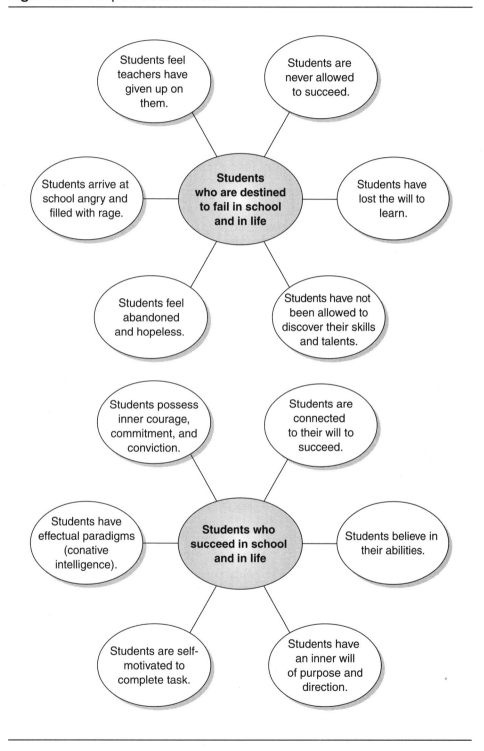

- visualize relationships using existing knowledge, and
- draw their own conclusions (Perkins, 1992; Pressley et al., 1992).

When we encourage students to develop learning, we also help them analyze the effectiveness of the strategies they choose to reach their goals. When students realize that their thoughts control their actions (i.e., that their locus of control is internal), they can positively affect their own beliefs and academic performance.

Figure 2.4   Semantic Web for Examining Your Values

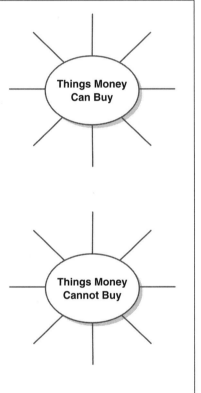

1. Use the semantic web to the right to brainstorm all the things that you believe would enrich your life or make you happy if you had money to buy them.

2. Select four items from your web and answer the following questions in one or two short paragraphs:

   - How did you narrow your list to these four items?
   - Why do you feel or think these things could enrich your life or make you happy?
   - How do you plan to obtain the money that will enable you to buy all of the things your heart desires?

3. Use the semantic web to the right to brainstorm all the things that would enrich your life that money *cannot* buy.

4. Select four items from your web and answer the following questions in one or two short paragraphs:

   - How did you narrow your list to these four items?
   - Why do you feel or think these things could enrich your life or make you happy?
   - Why do you feel that money is not necessary to enrich your life or make you happy?

5. Compare your list with those of your peers and discuss your selections and reasons.

ACHIEVING HIGH PERFORMANCE IN SPITE OF THE ODDS

Without energy and will, high performance cannot be achieved. When we push beyond the façade of anger and emptiness that some reluctant

Figure 2.5   Sample Semantic Feature Analysis

(High School Level)
Know Your Leaders

Identify the people listed below according to their leadership style by placing an X in the appropriate box.

	Leader	President	Dictator	Religious Leader	Royalty	Other
Thomas Jefferson						
Louis XIV						
Mohandas Gandhi						
Ayatollah Khomeini						
Elizabeth 1						
Genghis Khan						
Golda Meir						
Joan of Arc						
Eleanor Roosevelt						
Adolf Hitler						
Ivan the Terrible						
Winston Churchill						
Julius Caesar						
Nelson Mandela						

learners express, we open them and ourselves to new possibilities and a future that perhaps they never would have known. People change when they feel they have hope. Is your classroom filled with hope? Is there anything that you can do to support the change you want to see in students who are not engaged in learning?

When we teach with conation in mind, we find that conation is its own reward. Conation enables learners to seek higher levels of learning while strengthening their courage and character. Actually, conation reveals who we truly are beneath the surface, and what we are truly made of in terms of energy, endurance, and fortitude.

The Will to Succeed

Learners driven to succeed will travel down roads that are not always smooth. They will sometimes acquire battle scars in order to overcome obstacles. However, the battle scars are evidence of the learners' courage to continue and not give up. Successful learners are sustained by the belief that they can succeed and do so as a result of internal volition (their own conative spirit) and encouraging beliefs held by teachers, parents, and significant others.

Our efforts to transform learning into high performance begins with our understanding of what makes learning happen—what brings about the *will* to learn, what creates the "buy-in," and what transforms a life. In our search to define success in academics and in life, we know that some students simply need to uncover within themselves the will and determination to learn and "to do." Who will show them? Who will teach them? Who will be there for them? The answer is we will! We teachers must be the leaders!

Through conation, goals are accomplished, success is achieved, results are attained, and intellectual effort is put forth. Every individual has the ability to take action. However, ability remains in the form of potential until knowledge and emotions are moved into productive action.

The conative world is multidimensional. It is the world of the mind and heart filled with internal cheerleaders, constructivists, and instructional bulldozers, all doing their part to level the intellectual playing field and to cheer the learner on to academic success and greatness. The victorious cheers that come from *within* guide students to fulfillment, purpose, and meaning in life. We must teach our young to be cognizant of the road signs, pay attention to detours and barriers, and instill in them the fact that they have the *knowledge, will, determination,* and *power* to successfully reach their destinations—if they put forth the effort.

Lessons From the Heart of Learning

Teachers, administrators, parents, and other stakeholders are aware of the fact that when a student has a sense of self-worth and confidence, they are better equipped to cope with academic and personal challenges that they are confronted with on a daily basis. They are able to deal with "uninviting" and sometimes hostile learning environments because they are aware of their intellectual strengths and have a firm belief in themselves, their values, and their abilities. However, some students may not be aware of their qualities until given the opportunity to reflect on and explore their inner essence.

The following lessons have been designed to help students think about their positive attributes, identify their strengths, recognize their abilities, and discover their individual skills, gifts, and talents. This process will help them understand they have the power and inner ability to succeed.

CONATIVE CHARACTER MAP

Nothing in this world can take the place of persistence. Talent will not; nothing is more common than unsuccessful people with talent.

—Calvin Coolidge

WHAT'S IT ALL ABOUT?

Grade Level: Elementary, Middle, and High School

Purpose

- To acquaint students with the elements of narrative and expository texts
- To develop an awareness of cultures, genders, and ethnicities through various characters and their traits
- To promote an understanding of the elements of character development through reading and writing activities
- To promote an understanding of one's ability to accomplish a desired goal in life
- To help students understand the power of the will

Instructional Objectives

- Students will develop an understanding of character traits and how these traits impact on one's life.
- Students will improve comprehension and critical thinking skills through an in-depth analysis of characters and their actions.
- Students will enhance their knowledge and understanding of characterization in fiction and nonfiction genres.
- Students will gain an understanding of cognitive, affective, and conative skills as they explore characters in various situations.

Interdisciplinary Implementation

- History
- Career education
- Language arts
- Technology
- Library science

Instructional Focus

Students will complete the Conative Character Map and will improve their abilities in

- making inferences,
- applying metacognition,
- accessing prior knowledge, and
- using critical thinking.

MAKING THE CONNECTION

Instructional Strategies and Activities

1. Ask students to work as individuals, in pairs, or in cooperative teams of three to five students.
2. Tell students to read a story, trade book, or novel about a person who achieved his or her goals through conation.
3. Challenge students to complete the Conative Character Map.

CONATIVE INSIGHT: Now that I know, what will I do?

Extended Research and Reflection

Help students reflect on their learning by discussing the following:

1. Did you acquire a better understanding of the character as you reflected on the traits, skills, and qualities of this person?
2. Explain your answer by giving examples from the story or incidents encountered by the character.

ASSESSMENT

Assess the success of the lesson by asking yourself the following questions:

1. Did students demonstrate interest in the reading assignment? How did they demonstrate their interest?
2. How did students demonstrate their understanding of the character and his or her actions?
3. Were students able to identify with the character personally or with someone they knew? How did they do this?
4. How effectively were students able to apply their metacognitive, literacy, and critical thinking skills? How was this evidenced?

5. Were students able to understand the underlying theme (persevering in spite of the odds)? How did each student evidence this?

Conative Character Map

2. How do you think the main character was able to accomplish the things he or she accomplished? Where do you think his or her strength of will and character came from?

1. List three character traits that prove the main character believed in him- or herself.

3. How do you think this story would have ended if the character did not have the will and determination to succeed?

8. Name at least two people who have been influential in your life and explain why you selected these two.

4. Write three things that demonstrate the main character had determination and the will to do whatever was required of him or her to achieve his or her goal.

7. Explain three things that give you the incentive to never give up your attempts to be successful.

5. Describe one way that you and the main character are similar.

6. Give two reasons why you know you are able to succeed in whatever you put your mind to do.

ONE, TWO, THREE, JUST TAKE A LOOK AT ME

Character is power.

—Booker T. Washington

WHAT'S IT ALL ABOUT?

Grade Level: Primary, Elementary, Middle, and High School

Purpose

- To develop students' recognition of numbers and number values
- To develop students' knowledge of math concepts
- To enhance students' awareness of their talents, skills, and special gifts
- To tap into students' multiple intelligences

Instructional Objectives

- Students will use their prior knowledge.
- Students will implement math concepts.
- Students will enrich their literacy skills.
- Students will enhance their self-esteem.

Interdisciplinary Implementation

- Mathematics
- Literacy
- Character education
- Technology

Instructional Focus

Students will utilize the **All About Me** completion sheet to

- consider how they perceive themselves,
- contemplate how they think others perceive them,
- think about their personal and academic abilities, and
- see how these qualities can help them be successful in school and life.

MAKING THE CONNECTION

Instructional Strategies and Activities

1. Select a story or book to read to the students that focuses on the main character's positive qualities, heroic actions, and belief in him- or herself.
2. Ask students to identify and discuss the following:
    a. Who is the main character?
    b. What does the character do that makes him or her special?
    c. Why is the character considered a hero, a nice person, or a special friend?
    d. How does the character help others and act considerate, smart, and successful?
    e. How does the character demonstrate a belief in him- or herself?
    f. How does the character use his or her determination to achieve whatever goal he or she has set?
3. Challenge students to complete the All About Me worksheet. Explain that students can use words or pictures to express their thoughts.

CONATIVE INSIGHT: Now that I know, what will I do?

Extended Research and Reflection

1. Have younger students read, watch a story video, or listen to a story about animals or people who have survived difficult situations or who have demonstrated their ability to endure and not give up.
2. Have students complete a story map to demonstrate their understanding.
3. Have older students do research on a nonfictional person who has exhibited having self-assurance, determination, and belief in themselves and their abilities.
4. Have students write a paper based on their research.

ASSESSMENT

Help students reflect upon the lesson by asking them the following questions:

1. Did these activities help you think about all of the character's good qualities?
2. Do you feel proud of who you are?

Assess the success of the lesson by asking yourself the following questions:

1. Did students gain an understanding of and enhance their knowledge about the sequence of numbers? How was this knowledge demonstrated?
2. Were students able to use their prior knowledge and various cognitive and creative skills with this activity? How?
3. Were students able to demonstrate their comprehension skills? How?

All About Me

My name is _____

1 One thing I like about myself is . . .

2 Two things my family likes about me are . . .

3 Three things I am really good at are . . .

4 Four things that make me the special person I am are . . .

5 Five things that help me succeed in school and outside of school are . . .

YOU ARE MORE THAN YOU THINK!

The Conative Connection

On the following pages, the concept of conation and its application to the instructional process of integrating reading, writing, and critical thinking skills with the domains of cognition and affection are demonstrated in the following instructional activities for middle and high school students. Bloom's Taxonomy is used as a construct to illustrate the application and relationship among the taxonomy levels and the cognitive, affective, and conative domains. In addition, note the levels of the taxonomy below, arranged from the lowest (knowledge) to the highest (evaluation), and their corresponding relationships to the three domains when applied to literature.

Levels of Bloom's Taxonomy

Knowledge → → → Gathering information, facts, data

Comprehension → → Understanding, confirming

Application → → → Demonstrating understanding through utilization

Analysis → → → Probing, examining, investigating

Synthesis → → → Pulling together of information, facts, and data

Evaluation → → → Judging, ascertaining, concluding

YOU ARE MORE THAN YOU THINK!

I have met my hero, and he is me.

—George Sheehan

WHAT'S IT ALL ABOUT

Grade Level: Middle and High School

Purpose

- To enhance students' critical thinking skills
- To encourage students to read good literature
- To help students better understand the relationship between and the interconnectiveness of the cognitive, affective, and conative domains

Instructional Objectives

- Students will be able to enhance their critical thinking skills.
- Students will improve their ability to think at higher levels, through effective questioning strategies.
- Students will be able to identify specific differences between the affective, cognitive, and conative domains.
- Students will reflect on, evaluate, and determine the talents, values, and convictions they possess.

Interdisciplinary Implementation

- English
- History
- Character education
- Technology
- Reading
- Critical thinking skills

Instructional Focus

The teacher will want to provide some historical background regarding the Holocaust in order to give students a foundational knowledge base of the time in which this story occurred. It is essential that students understand Anne Frank's story is nonfiction; she and her family actually experienced the events described in the book.

- Have students read *The Diary of Anne Frank.* (There are several versions available. Please select the one that is appropriate for the reading and comprehension abilities of your students.)
- Utilize the concept of literature circles (3–5 students) as they read and discuss the book.
- Have students complete the following activity in their literature circles or in cooperative teams.
- Allow time for students to engage in dialogue, providing thoughtful answers and a valid rationale for each of their responses. (Please be aware that this activity could expand over 2–3 days.)

MAKING THE CONNECTION

Instructional Strategies and Activities

The Diary of Anne Frank

Knowledge

Cognitive: Who was Anne Frank?

RESPONSE:

Affective: Give two examples that demonstrate Anne was a typical teenager.

RESPONSE:

Conative: How did Anne's father overcome the barrier of her not being allowed to attend the regular town school?

RESPONSE:

Comprehension

Cognitive: Which historical situation was developing at the time of Anne's young life?

RESPONSE:

Affective: Did the developing events change the family ties of Anne and her parents? Give an example to prove your answer.

RESPONSE:

Conative: What do you think gave Anne and her family the strength and ability to cope with their changing world?

RESPONSE:

Application

Cognitive: What were some clues that indicated the drastic changes to come for the Jewish people?

RESPONSE:

Affective: Describe how you would have felt if you had been in Anne's situation.

RESPONSE:

Conative: What do you think gave Anne the courage to continue to try having a normal life?

RESPONSE:

Analysis

Cognitive: Why do you think Anne recorded the daily events of her life?

RESPONSE:

Affective: Why do you think people hate others who are different? How do you think this problem can be solved?

RESPONSE:

Conative: List three character traits Anne possessed that gave her the will to live.

RESPONSE:

Synthesis

Cognitive: How do you think Anne's life would have been different had she not been Jewish?

RESPONSE:

Affective: If she had a choice, do you think Anne would have changed her ethnicity? Why or why not?

RESPONSE:

Conative: Have you ever, or have you known someone who has, faced certain prejudices because of race or religion? Write about this experience.

RESPONSE:

Evaluation

Cognitive: Why do you think the Jewish people were targeted for persecution?

RESPONSE:

Affective: Throughout history, different people have suffered cruel and unjust punishment because they were the "wrong" color, sex, or religion. Find an example in a book or story and write about it. Tell how the story or book made you feel.

RESPONSE:

Conative: Read another book or story about a character(s) who exhibited conative traits. What was it that motivated this person, and others like them, to accomplish seemingly impossible feats or have the courage, spirit, perseverance, and *will* to do the things they did in the face of harsh adversities?

RESPONSE:

CONATIVE INSIGHT: Now that I know, what will I do?

Extended Research and Reflection

Have the students use the Lexicon on pages 147–148 to select five characteristics that describe the type of person Anne Frank was. Then have them select five characteristics that describe the other person or character they read about.

Have them use the **Compare and Contrast** chart to make a comparison between these two individuals.

Compare and Contrast

Characters:	Anne Frank	Selected Character
Attribute #1:		
Attribute #2:		
Attribute #3:		
Attribute #4:		
Attribute #5:		

1. Instruct students to write a descriptive paragraph that is a summarization of the information in their chart.
2. Direct students to pair with a friend or classmate and duplicate this activity.
3. Have a reflective discussion session on how students perceived themselves.

ASSESSMENT

1. Have students form cooperative teams of three to five, depending on number of students in the class. Each team will refer back to the various characters selected in the **Extended Research and Reflection section.**
2. Each team will develop six questions; one question for each level of Bloom's Taxonomy, related to their selected characters.
3. Each team will present their questions. The class will determine, through discussion and comparions, if the level of questions developed applies to level of difficulty, especially for "application, analysis, synthesis, and evalution." (Having the students utilize overhead transparencies on which to write their questions would be most effective.)
4. Discuss the difference between simple, literal questions and more difficult ones. Remind students that: "Responding to a simple question does not require much thinking; however, in order to adequately respond to a difficult question requires one to think!" This develops their critical thinking skills that will help them in their other classes and life in general.

3

Where Learning Lives

Instructional Strategies That Engage Students

When I think about one of the best lessons I learned in school so far, it is the lesson that "being me" is okay. Just being me was always hard, because everyone used to doubt me and tell me I would never be anything in life. Finding myself took a lot of work and courage. It took time to find out what I was good at and what I needed help with. In the seventh grade, my teacher told me, "Don't ever let anyone doubt you because you are an intelligent young lady." Since then, I took that to heart, forgetting about everyone that doubted me, telling myself that I could be anything I want to be in life. That's why being me is the best thing I learned.

—Elementary student

Creating an environment that encourages risk-taking and positive attitudes toward one another, as well as with oneself, begins when the students enter the classroom on the first day of school. As my students create a classroom "bill of rights," they realize they are being empowered with the ability to control their own destiny. They will be making choices that will affect them as learners, friends, and most importantly, as individuals. This enhances their inner will to think positively about themselves. To reinforce this thought we have our classroom motto, **"If I Think I Can, I Can!,"** *which is said after the pledge and is displayed in the room as a banner.*

The students know I will not give up on them and they cannot give up on themselves! I know we have succeeded when students encourage one another in the classroom by saying, "You can do it!" or "If you think you can do it, you will." This wonderful encouragement demonstrates an intrinsic understanding of believing in oneself and processing the will to try.

—High school teacher

WHAT IS LEARNING?

Authentic learning is a conscious exercise, starting with who we are and evolving into all that we become. In order for students to succeed in academics (or in life), they first need help in discovering the ability to learn within themselves. Second, they must acquire or build their courage to learn.

"The Thinking Curriculum" (NCREL) defines learning as "the active, goal-directed construction of meaning. This definition of learning takes a constructive, perceptive, metacognitive, connective, and transformative view." The Greek definition for education is leading another out of darkness or ignorance. To set the learning process in motion, the teacher must have the desire to lead. The foundation of teaching is the simple, yet powerful, belief that one can teach and others can learn. Teachers have the ability to foster students' learning and build their courage to learn through everyday lessons in regular classrooms. We call this authentic teaching and learning.

The Will to Succeed

Leading the Way
Teachers and mentors are on the cutting edge of students' lives. Teachers are the ones who will lead the way, who open students' hearts as well as their minds. When our young rise, the world will note that their success was cultivated by how we chose to be their examples—what we chose to be to them and for them.

Learning in the Conative Domain

Over the past two decades, we've discovered much about the way the brain learns. For example, we know that the brain makes meaning by finding connections and that emotions play a large role in memory and recall (Wolfe, 2001). In addition to what we've learned about brain physiology, we've also learned about how the brain works through the study of conation. For example, we know that before learning takes place, two things must happen: The learner must choose to learn and the learner must have enough courage to make the choice to learn. Making the choice to learn is influenced by the learner's perception of herself, her perception of the world around her, her beliefs, how she interprets what she knows or thinks she knows, and how she chooses to respond to what she believes. Perseverance is the single most important conative component. Figure 3.1 offers a number of reflection questions that can be used at different stages of learning. You and your students may use these questions to reflect upon how you perceive the role of perseverance in your own lives. Questions that raise issues of right vs. wrong or right vs. right are questions that involve ethical decision-making and fall into the domain of *metaconation.*

Figure 3.1   The Perserverance Factor

- Am I willing to persevere to learn?
- Am I persevering?
- Why am I persevering?
- How have I changed as a result of my perseverance?
- Next steps?

Beneath a question is not always an answer but perhaps another question–more powerful than the one preceding it. Pushing for answers in a classroom is not always the issue. Students often learn on much deeper levels when given time to ponder thoughtful considerations that seek depth and richness.

Choice in a Conative Context

Sometimes the conative difference between choosing for or against learning, living, and succeeding lies simply in giving oneself permission to learn, grow, and become. Our challenge is to help students make the conative connection by using realistic, yet challenging, goals and strategies that foster students' desire to learn.

The greater the correlation between one's personal want or need to know and one's willingness to learn a particular concept or subject, the stronger the possibility that the task will be attempted and possibly learned. Kohl (1991) maintains that some students make a conscious decision not to learn and that these students present an intellectual and social challenge. These would-be learners—those who are not yet interested nor committed to studying—are kept out of the learning game by default. Unfortunately, they are often also left out of the rigors of the game of life as well.

Personal belief and willingness are elemental and relational factors that tend to promote or inhibit one's desire to strive. These two factors, belief and willingness, are affective and conative variables that play a significant role in learning. One's choice to enter the learning process and then involve oneself in the pursuit of learning requires personal and academic commitment. A belief in one's ability to learn and a willingness to participate in the act of learning as a means to achieve a specific goal are the first steps on the journey that leads to authentic success.

Teachers should help students become aware that they must make an affirmative choice to learn. Teachers can use Your Conative Profile, found in the Resources section of this book, to help students recognize the connection between will and success. The lesson at the end of this chapter titled "If I Had a Choice, I Would Be . . . " can also help students harness the power of conation.

After making the choice to learn, the learner must amass the courage to act on the choice. The next section discusses the role of courage in the learning process.

WHAT IS COURAGE?

Courage is *wisdom* connected to *will*. This connection sparks action. Whether or not an individual decides to act is dependent upon that individual's

- belief,
- knowledge,
- wisdom, and
- will.

Belief. Simply put, belief is accepting as true something for which there may or may not be subjective proof. The beliefs we hold, whether deliberately chosen or instilled, create a model for interpreting and structuring our perception of what is real and what we can do as a result.

Knowledge. Today, the meaning of the word *knowledge* is debatable. For the sake of this discussion, knowledge is a collection of information. Each piece of information is a facet through which the world is perceived by a particular individual.

Wisdom. We can think of wisdom as being synonymous with sound judgment. Wisdom provides responsible direction to the will. In other words, wisdom, when infused with will, leads to responsible action.

If the action of the will proceeds without wisdom, negative outcomes may be the result. Wisdom sets the direction and it positions learning at the center of action. Acting with wisdom (good judgment) lifts us up by strengthening our determination and by helping us interpret our life experiences. Acting with a lack of wisdom holds us back.

Will (conation). When we look at the role of the will in terms of courage (or lack of courage), we discover that our courage is affected by what we believe about ourselves and how we interpret life experiences and the world around us. Being courageous depends on what we choose to believe. For our purposes, the will moves knowledge from thought to action.

Why focus on the will? The will is the center of action and behavior. Through our will, the world discovers who we truly are and how we've combined our beliefs, knowledge, and (hopefully) wisdom and directed them toward productive goals. We will examine the impact of these four factors and others when looking more closely at what moves individuals toward or away from a specific goal in Chapter 4.

The Will to Succeed

The Power Within

What this power is, I cannot say. All I know is that it exists . . . and it becomes available only when you are in that state of mind in which you know exactly what you want and are fully determined not to quit until you get it.

—Alexander Graham Bell

GHOLAR AND RIGGS' CONATIVE TAXONOMY

For decades, researchers have relied on Bloom's taxonomy (Bloom et al., 1956), an instructional tool designed to allow teachers to determine the six levels of higher-order thinking skills. In comparison, we have created a conative taxonomy, an evaluative tool designed to enable teachers to assess levels of student engagement in the learning process. The fundamental framework for the conative taxonomy of self-directed learning includes these elements: *personal discovery, transition, transformation,* and *transcendency.* These elements are described in Figure 3.2.

Students engage or disengage their will to learn based on their perception of reality. Students want to know: "What's in it for me?" If they feel or believe that learning is worth their effort, they will put forth the effort and more, sometimes exceeding established goals.

Authentic Success

Authentic teaching and learning produces an educational environment wherein students are seldom solely motivated to perform with the promise of material rewards. The challenge of achieving a task becomes its own reward. Authentic learning occurs in the conative domain. Learning is perceived as relevant, important, and full of meaning. Students stretch, grow, and move beyond their prior limits. The development of their perceptual capacity tends to increase. They see themselves as capable and make observable movement toward mutually shared goals. Figure 3.3

Figure 3.2   Gholar and Riggs' Conative Taxonomy

Transcendency

At this level students and teachers possess the will to

- give voice to ideas and issues that matter most;
- rise above old paradigms that are no longer useful;
- take an ethical stand in uncomfortable situations;
- encourage others to strive, believe, and release the past (if necessary) in order to renew their relationships with learning and life; and
- be a light in dark places.

Transformation

At this level students and teachers possess the will to

- live fully and become their personal best,
- increase positive learning experiences,
- experience learning as its own personal reward, and
- transform knowledge into wisdom.

Transition

At this level students and teachers possess the will to

- engage fully in learning,
- change,
- focus and remain focused on an expected goal,
- produce quality work (students) and quality teaching experiences (teachers), and
- open themselves to authentic learning and teaching.

Personal discovery

At this level students and teachers possess the will to

- value themselves as learners (students) or leaders (teachers),
- value learning,
- *see* beyond today,
- succeed, and
- appreciate themselves through their own eyes.

Figure 3.3   Authentic Success—Connecting Learning to Living

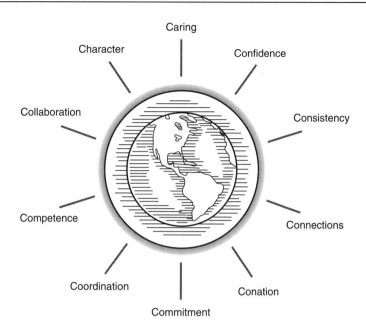

shows the characteristics of authentic learning that help students succeed in school and in life.

CONATION AND CHARACTER BUILDING: THE STRENGTH AND SPIRIT OF LEARNING

During childhood, students acquire the bricks and mortar to fashion the foundation for character building. This foundation will serve them throughout their lives. If the edifice is solid, students will thrive. They will learn, grow, and become responsible individuals who demonstrate courage, respect, and integrity.

Parents are a child's first and most significant character educators. Whether modeling the Golden Rule, emphasizing the importance of honesty, demonstrating the power of perseverance by staying with a task until it is done, or showing concern for those less fortunate, most parents try their best to teach their sons and daughters the essential lessons of character.

Some believe the distance between the learners and the expectations that have been established for their learning are simply too far apart, unattainable, and unrealistic. As facilitators of learning, our role is to teach, and our conative role is to teach students how to shorten this distance. We can do so by being external cheerleaders, thus encouraging students to become their own internal cheerleaders. Through literature, technology, videos, movies, and other experiences, we can teach students how they can fight and win battles, especially battles to overcome the odds in school, and most importantly, in life.

WHAT IS CHARACTER?

A popular definition of character is "what we do when no one else is around." We often think that a person's character is "tested" in response to various challenges, temptations, or ethical dilemmas. (For example, we determine we won't cheat even when no one else is around.) Other definitions refer to character as a moral compass or one's capacity to draw the line where none exists.

Character, from the Greek word *charakter*, has come to mean the constellation of strengths and weaknesses that form and reveal who we are. Our character does not consist of a single statement or a random act of generosity, but it comprises our everyday qualities and dispositions—both good and bad. Assessing our character involves taking an inventory of what we spend most of our time thinking about and doing.

CHARACTER DEVELOPMENT

Sometimes called social and emotional learning (SEL; ASCD, 1997), character education provides lessons in character building. These practices have the potential to transform ethical ambiguity into ethical clarity and moral action. Service learning, mentoring, peer mediation, and student leadership are among the programs that successfully increase students' social and emotional intelligence (Barr & Parrett, 2003; ASCD, 1997). Education emphasizes the responsibilities and benefits of productive living in a global and diverse society. Character education prepares students to come face-to-face with the realities of life and equips them with the tools they need to make ethically sound decisions and responsible choices in a world of challenge, opportunity, and change.

SEL program emphasis is on developing key social skills to enable students to be responsible and become community-concerned citizens. For many students, school is where socialization takes place. Therefore, it is the school's responsibility to observe and incorporate skills and strategies for understanding the emotional way students interact with their classroom environment. In addition, SEL is a process that includes strategies to enhance and enforce student's emotional health, ethical, and academic learning within the classroom. These strategies look at the whole picture of how cognitive and social skills are linked to create the optimal learning experience. (Based on a research paper written by Dahlia Refai, graduate student of Loyola University, Chicago, 2007).

These practices have the potential to transform ethical ambiguity into ethical clarity and moral action.

Making Heartfelt Connections

In the conative domain, we engage students in realizing their dreams by bolstering their courage and their will to learn. We help students strive for success by giving light and sharing personal meaning as they move forward on the path to knowledge.

Academic success is embodied in the will to learn—to know, strive, believe, interact, initiate, risk, respond, and fully engage in the process of learning. Courageous teaching involves the same connections. We need connections that matter, connections that are heartfelt. We need to connect (or reconnect) to our ideals. We can connect by engaging in human moments, moments that occur when two individuals pay attention to one another.

The Will to Succeed

Courage, Character, and Conation

The stamp of conscience is the will. Our identity resides in what we value—what we believe is just, true, fair, responsible, and good for all individuals. Our identity is imprinted by our courage, character, and conation. Courage, character, and conation help us to make a difference and make our presence felt through positive contributions to our world. These qualities bring us together. They make us one.

Do we need courage? Do we need character? Do we need conation? Each generation answers these questions in their own way. We teach our students the importance of these values by the way we live, by our daily interactions with them, by the verbal and nonverbal messages they receive from us.

A majority of Americans share a respect for the fundamental traits of character—honesty, compassion, justice, courage, generosity, perseverance, self-discipline, responsibility, respect, and caring. Yet, in contemporary culture, many of our youth feel uncertain when faced with issues of right and wrong. Young people have even more difficulty when faced with choices at a higher level of decision-making—when they must choose between right and right. Ambiguous actions on the part of youth and an inability to understand or care about relationships or the human condition are in themselves ethical dilemmas. Harvard scholar and psychologist Robert Coles (1997) postulates that children possess an innate desire to learn the difference between right and wrong and to observe models of moral behavior. Students look to the adults in their lives for wisdom, hope, and meaning.

Through character education, students gain insight into what is important and what is not. As they make choices and seek to fulfill their dreams, students learn to respect themselves, others, and the world around them. When taught to live their lives in an ethical manner they develop resilience and a sense of purpose. Lessons taught at home stay with students as they make their way through school and life.

Flight Training

In conative classrooms, teaching and learning are like flight training—students learn to take off with new ideas. Teachers who are inspired to continue their own journeys lift students' minds and hearts and motivate them to achieve to their highest potential. As students become more self-confident and willing to be persistent in their academic studies, they climb to higher and higher take off points. As they become more and more willing to learn and grow, they take off and fly. Conation, courage, and character—in one voice, together we speak!

WHEN CONATION, COURAGE, AND CHARACTER BECOME ONE

Conation is the inspiration that changes the way we see ourselves in the world and ways we propose to live our lives

—Cheryl Gholar

Conation is part of a greater whole, a continuum that leads to metaconation™. Just as conation is referenced as goal-oriented action, metaconation is distinguished by being goal-oriented action *guided by ethical decision-making*. The metaconative domain is referred to on page 10. Two examples of metaconation are on pages 81, 136, and 137. A person who demonstrates metaconation displays moral courage and action in the face of ethical challenges, does "the right thing even if it's not popular," and refuses to stand by idly while others engage in unethical or harmful behavior.

Metaconation is not a complicated concept to explain. It's ethical action directed toward achieving the highest good. It's about becoming and living the best of your highest self. Moral courage is the hallmark of metaconation. When taught and experienced as a way to operationalize one's life, students and teachers can reach higher levels of knowing and being. As global citizens, "no culture that we know lacks the notions of good and bad or true and false," says British intellectual Isiah Berlin. He singles out courage as an example of a universal value that, as far as we can tell, has been admired in every society known to us.

Courage as a value is growing in public favor throughout American culture. A casual mention of the need for *ethics* according to Rushworth Kidder brings knowing nods. A mention of the need for *moral courage* can bring people to their feet in enthusiastic agreement. Metaconation is ethical action at its highest level. The litmus test for each of us as individuals and collectively as a society will be found in the choices we make with the knowledge we will acquire through formal and informal education. The beliefs we uphold and act upon will be the result of how we interpret our relationships and learning experiences over the span of our lives.

Conation and metaconation are unique parts of the same whole, guiding human behavior through a working continuum that builds success and significance in education. A culture that encourages metaconation as a way of being in the world is one of the noblest goals of a civil society. As a global community and a nation of nations, we can surpass the ordinary and share our world in remarkable ways. We can rise as one in mindful celebration of the gifts we can offer to the singularity of humanity.

Conation, metaconation, courage, integrity, and character are part of a purposeful synergy that enables us to question and move against the odds. What do we know for sure and what are we willing to do to make certain that those things in life which are precious and good are protected? What role will we play in ensuring their opportunity to grow and flourish? Among the questions that awaken us to discover our purpose, we don't always find answers—but richer, deeper questions to ponder and respond to.

Lessons From the Heart of Learning

Students are sometimes overlooked as individuals who have strong feelings and emotions, as well as hopes and dreams. Many of them conceal their hurt and pain because they feel adults will not understand or simply do not care. They often hesitate to take the risk of sharing their aspirations for fear of being ridiculed.

The heart of learning lives in the hearts of learners. The heart of teaching resides in the hearts of those who teach. When the opening of the two unfolds in the classroom, something happen—something changes. The internal force that builds meaning and hope rises and the process of learning begins.

The following lessons encourage students to explore and express their emotions through positive and creative channels. Through these activities, they are urged to reflect on their challenges and/or think about the future, while keeping in mind that they have the talents, skills, and will to overcome adversities.

IT'S NOT ALWAYS WHAT IT SEEMS TO BE!

You see it's like a portmanteau—there are two meanings packed into one word.

—Lewis Carroll

WHAT'S IT ALL ABOUT

Grade Level: Middle and High School

Purpose

- To enhance understanding of metaphors
- To promote creative writing through the use of metaphors
- To use personal experiences and knowledge as a foundation for creating poems and compositions

Instructional Objectives

- Students will learn how to use metaphors.
- Students will strengthen their writing and higher-order thinking skills.
- Students will acquire new vocabulary words.

Interdisciplinary Implementation

- Language arts
- Social studies
- Science

Instructional Focus

Students will learn about metaphors and will read the poem "Song of a Dandelion" and reflect upon the following questions:

- Do you think the student poet was writing about dandelions? Why or why not?
- What message is the author trying to convey through metaphor?
- Is it easier to express emotions using metaphors?

MAKING THE CONNECTION

Instructional Strategies and Activities

1. Discuss and define the word *metaphor.* Explain that authors use metaphors to make stories and poetry more interesting and fun to read.

2. Place students in teams of three to five students. To ensure that students understand the concept of a metaphor, challenge them to think of a few examples of metaphors with their teams. Stress that the metaphors can be about anything in their lives or personal experiences or can even center around their subjects in school, such as language arts, science, and math. Following are some sample metaphors:

   - Algebra is a bone-crushing headache.
   - The color blue is a cool, refreshing wave on the hottest day of the year.
   - The human brain is a computer with an infinite amount of memory.
   - The character's mouth was a garbage can.

3. Encourage teams to share their metaphors. As teams share, ask the class to interpret the meaning of each metaphor.

4. Continue the dialogue about the usage of metaphors, providing additional examples if needed.

5. Encourage students to silently re-read the poem "Song of a Dandelion Pushing up Through an Urban Sidewalk Crack."

6. Ask students:

   a. Do you think the author was writing only about dandelions?

   b. Could this poem be a metaphor about something or someone else?

Call students' attention to specific lines or words in the poem (e.g., "No other flowers can mimic our style" or "atmosphere" or other significant words or phrases). Students will likely be able to conclude that this poem could be about homeless or economically disadvantaged people or students who are not smart, attractive, or popular.

Song of a Dandelion Pushing up
Through an Urban Sidewalk Crack

We sprout up boldly through the cracks to offer beauty that the sidewalk lacks.

And spread our sunshine-bright yellow smiles.

No other flowers can mimic our style.

They call us weeds, but we are a gift sent from heaven to brighten and uplift the sad, gray atmosphere.

No other flowers dare to grow around here.

If you would stop and simply see our beauty compared to the misery . . . the dirt and pieces of broken glass and useless things that litter the grass,

You would not see us as simply weeds, but as beings that a city needs.

Yes, we smile defiantly anyway, and flash our smile to boldly display what joy can come from the little things.

We are a song, and if you listen, we sing.

—High school student

CONATIVE INSIGHT: Now that I *know*, what will I do?

Extended Research and Reflection

Challenge each team to create a metaphor that focuses on a social issue or some topic of interest to them. Tell teams to create a story or poem based on the metaphor they created. Encourage teams to share their poems or stories with the class.

Ask Students

- To share positive ways to express frustration
- What characters in movies, novels, or plays that they are familiar with have shown perseverance?

Assessment

Assess the success of the lesson by asking yourself the following questions:

1. Did students demonstrate their understanding of metaphors? How?
2. Were students able to work cooperatively in teams to develop their poems or stories? How was this cooperation demonstrated?
3. Did students exhibit creativity and critical thinking skills? How?
4. Were students able to demonstrate their knowledge of strategies for dealing with difficult situations?

IF I HAD A CHOICE, I WOULD BE . . .

A failure establishes only this, that our determination to succeed was not strong enough.

—John Christian Bovee

WHAT'S IT ALL ABOUT

Grade Level: Elementary, Middle, and High School

Purpose

- To enhance students' awareness of their creative abilities
- To tap into students' multiple intelligences
- To probe students' prior knowledge of science concepts

Instructional Objectives

- Students will use their prior knowledge.
- Students will implement math and science concepts.
- Students will enhance their literacy skills.
- Students will develop their comprehension skills.

Interdisciplinary Implementation

- Science
- Language arts
- Vocabulary
- Technology

Instructional Focus

Students will read *The Very Hungry Caterpillar* by Eric Carle and reflect upon the following issues:

- If you had the choice to do or be anything, what would you do or be?
- Why would you choose to do that?
- Can you attain this if you put all your effort into it?

MAKING THE CONNECTION

Instructional Strategies and Activities

1. Begin by reading the book *The Very Hungry Caterpillar* or a similar story. Read the title of the book, show students the cover, and ask inferential and comprehension questions such as:
   - What do you think this story is going to be about?
   - Is a caterpillar an animal or an insect?
   - Can you name some other kinds of insects?
   - Who can describe what a caterpillar looks like?
   - Has anyone ever held a caterpillar? How does it feel?

2. Read the story aloud. When you are finished reading, ask students these questions:
   - Do you think the caterpillar was happy being a caterpillar? Why or why not?
   - What do you think the caterpillar might want to be if he could be something different? Explain why.
   - Are you happy being who you are? Why or why not?

3. Divide the class into four cooperative teams. Encourage each team to select two choices from If I Had a Choice (on the following page). Ask teams to draw pictures of their selections.

4. When students have completed their drawings, challenge each team to do the following:
   - Tell why you chose your two insects.
   - Describe the insects you chose.
   - Explain all you know about your insects.
   - Display your drawings.

CONATIVE INSIGHT: Now that I *know*, what will I do?

Extended Research and Reflection

Challenge teams to select one of their insects and complete a Venn diagram, comparing and contrasting the differences and similarities between their insect and another team's insect. Provide appropriate grade-level science books or Internet resources available to aid the students.

Example: Compare and contrast a praying mantis and a wasp.

A. Three different characteristics of a praying mantis.

B. Three different characteristics of a wasp.

C. Three characteristics that are alike for both

If I Had a Choice, I Would Be . . .

If I had a choice, I would be an *ant*, because

_____ .

_____ .

If I had a choice, I would be a *butterfly*, because

_____ .

_____ .

If I had a choice, I would be a *honeybee*, because

_____ .

_____ .

If I had a choice, I would be a *caterpillar*, because

_____ .

_____ .

If I had a choice, I would be a *mosquito*, because

_____ .

_____ .

If I had a choice, I would be an *earthworm*, because

_____ .

_____ .

If I had a choice, I would be a *spider*, because

_____ .

_____ .

If I had a choice, I would be a *fly*, because

_____ .

_____ .

ASSESSMENT

Ask students the following questions so they may reflect upon what they learned in this lesson.

- Did this lesson help you learn more about insects? How?
- Did this lesson help you learn more about yourself? How?

Assess the success of the lesson by asking yourself the following questions:

- Did students gain an understanding of and enhance their knowledge about insects?
- How was this knowledge attainment determined?
- Were students able to use their prior knowledge and various cognitive and creative skills with this activity? How?
- Were students able to demonstrate their comprehension skills? How?

WHERE THERE IS A WILL, THERE IS HOPE

Fall down seven times; get up eight.

—Japanese Proverb

WHAT'S IT ALL ABOUT?

Grade Levels: Middle and High School

Purpose

- To expose students to the concept of cultural diversity
- To help students understand that people from different ethnic backgrounds also face adversities
- To help students understand people from different ethnic groups and cultures are more alike than different in many aspects

Instructional Objectives

- Students will become familiar with the trials, tribulations, and hardships experienced by individuals from other ethnic groups.
- Students will enhance their research skills.
- Students will enhance their reading, writing, and oral presentation styles.
- Students will develop an appreciation for "everyday heroes."
- Students will develop a better understanding of what it means "to have the will to persevere."

Interdisciplinary Implementation

- History
- Social Studies
- English
- Geography
- Research

Instructional Focus

- The teacher will select a story, newspaper article, or information from a television news report about an individual of any ethnic group, who came from another country where he or she suffered some type of persecution, but was able to persevere.
- The class will discuss the details of the story or article.

- Share the story with students, focusing on the details of what this person endured during this difficult time. The persecution could have been the result of religious, political, or "ethnic cleansing."

MAKING THE CONNECTION

Instructional Strategies and Activities

- Have the class do a research project, looking for similar stories of people from different ethnic backgrounds and write a report on their findings.
- The research project can be conducted by cooperative teams, pairs of students, or by individuals
- Share the following example with students to ensure they understand the expectations of this research project.

Example

Share the story of Mr. Siath Hen, of Asian Pacific heritage, who works as mental health counselor, serving Cambodian immigrants and refugees, many who suffered greatly during the Khmer Rouge regime. He, too, experienced the horrors of this regime, as his wife and four of his children were killed. However, in spite of this, he managed to find the will to persevere ("pick up the pieces" of his life) and commit to or dedicate his life to helping others.

To aid in guiding the direction of the research project, have students address the following questions:

- Who is the subject of your research?
- Why did you select this person?
- What is the ethnic or cultural background of your research subject?
- What country was the original home of your subject?
- What incidents or events happened that caused your subject to leave his or her homeland?
- How was your subject directly affected? (Was he or she tortured, imprisoned, lose family members?)
- How was your subject able to survive, persevere, or manage to survive?
- What character traits would you attribute to your subject and how did these traits contribute to his or her survival?
- What is your subject doing now?

CONATIVE INSIGHT: Now that I *know*, what will I do?

Extended Research and Reflections

Have students share their projects orally. Ask the following questions:

- What did you learn about people of other ethnicities and cultures that you did not know before doing this project?
- Did you learn more than information about your subject? For example, information about the geographical area where your subject lived, the political climate, etc. Were you surprised at what you learned? Explain.
- Do you think the key to your subject's survival was his or her courage, determination, and/or will to persevere? Explain.

ASSESSMENT

Informal: The reflective questions will serve as the assessment.

IF YOU THINK YOU CAN, YOU CAN!

Without conation there is no product, only potential.

—Ernestine Riggs

WHAT'S IT ALL ABOUT?

Grade Level: Elementary, Middle, and High School

Purpose

- To become acquainted with the contributions to our society by individuals of various genders, cultures, and ethnicities
- To become aware of stereotypical attitudes
- To promote an understanding of one's ability to accomplish a desired goal in life
- To understand the power of the will

Instructional Objectives

- Students will develop independent research skills.
- Students will acquire and enhance comprehension, inference, and critical thinking skills.
- Students will gain knowledge of fiction and nonfiction historical events through biographies, narrative, and expository text.
- Students will utilize metacognitive skills.
- Students will gain an understanding of cognitive, affective, and conative skills.

Interdisciplinary Implementation

- History
- Language arts
- Library science
- Career education
- Technology

Instructional Focus

Students will read the biography of Elizabeth Blackwell and reflect on the following issues:

- Historical context or time period
- Society's attitudes about women, their roles, and their capabilities
- Women's attitudes and perceptions about their roles and capabilities

MAKING THE CONNECTION

Instructional Strategies and Activities

1. Place students in cooperative teams of three to five students.
2. Ask students to read the biography of Elizabeth Blackwell.
3. Challenge each team to complete a character trait web for Elizabeth. Explain that the web should list all of her attributes, skills, and talents.
4. Encourage each team to share and compare their webs. Explain that each team should give a rationale for each trait they attributed to Dr. Blackwell.
5. Discuss the following questions with students:

   a. What do you think the statement "a socially prominent family" means?
   b. Why do you think Elizabeth did not want to conform to being a socially acceptable young lady?
   c. Would she be considered a nonconformist in today's society? Why or why not? Explain your response.
   d. What qualities or character traits do you think one would need to possess to be considered a "gracious lady" in the 1800s?
   e. Do you think the same qualities or character traits would apply now? Why or why not? Explain your response.
   f. Why do you think the Geneva Medical School accepted Elizabeth, while others rejected her application?
   g. Why do you think Elizabeth was persistent in her quest to become a doctor?
   h. Identify at least four qualities or character traits Elizabeth possessed that enabled her to never give up her dream of becoming a doctor.

Elizabeth Blackwell

Elizabeth Blackwell was born in 1821 into a socially prominent family. She was considered to be of "good breeding." Elizabeth did all of the social things expected of the young ladies in her position during this time period in history. However, she decided that she wanted her life to have more meaning than that of being a gracious lady who spent her days and evenings attending tea parties and other social events.

One of Elizabeth's friends, who understood Elizabeth's desire to do something useful with her life, suggested that Elizabeth go into the field of medicine. After much thought, Elizabeth decided to take a bold step and become a doctor. This was indeed a brave venture, because during this time, medicine was considered a man's domain. In fact, Elizabeth had to apply to several medical schools before she was finally accepted by the Geneva Medical School of New York. Needless to say, she had to face many hardships as she worked to complete her degree, but she persevered.

In 1849 she completed her training, graduated as the top student in her class, and became the first woman doctor in the United States. Her training served her country well, for when the Civil War began, she established a school to train nurses. These nurses treated and saved the lives of countless Union soldiers who were wounded in battle. She was the catalyst for other training programs that resulted in the availability of competent trained nurses for the Union army.

Elizabeth Blackwell died in 1910. She will always be remembered for her determination to become what she saw as her dream, in spite of what society had predestined for her. She practiced her right to be an individual and not only followed her dream, but turned that dream into a reality.

CONATIVE INSIGHT: Now that I *know*, what will I do?

Extended Research and Reflection

Encourage students to use the Internet to conduct research on the Geneva Medical School. Ask students to uncover the philosophy of the founders, the school's beliefs about the rights of women, the history of its admissions policy, the status of the school today, etc.

1. Encourage students to read, interpret, and discuss the following quote: "Whenever there is a human being, I see God-given rights inherent in that being whatever may be the sex or complexion." —William Lloyd Garrison
2. Ask students to reflect on the question: What character traits, self-perceptions, or values do you have that will enable you to face and overcome challenges in school and life?

ASSESSMENT

Assess the success of the lesson by asking yourself the following questions:

1. Did students exhibit comprehension skills? How?
2. How well did students demonstrate their research skills?
3. Did students demonstrate the ability to work cooperatively in teams? How?
4. Were students able to apply literacy skills and critical thinking skills effectively? How was this evidenced?
5. Were students able to understand the underlying theme of being able to persevere in spite of the odds? How was this evidenced by each student?

4

An Invitation to Learn

Awakening and Motivating Your Classroom

My teacher believes in me. She says encouraging things to me every day. I have the kind of teacher who makes all of the students in our class want to learn. She's really quite funny, but she also gets down to business. I'm always learning something new. It's great that she knows how to make learning fun. I scored well on my Iowa Test.

—Third-grade student

Caring is one of the most indefinable personal qualities, but it is one of the most important for a teacher.

—High school teacher

Students are acutely aware of what Dewey (1933) called the "hidden curriculum" that stems from classroom interactions between teachers and students and between students and other students. When these interactions are characterized by safety, cooperation, and respect, the learning environment tends to be inviting, welcoming, and stimulating. The environment also promotes conation and self-recognition.

INVITING SUCCESS

Inviting success begins with a clear understanding of issues, challenges, questions, and choices that students face daily at school and in the community. Many educators (and others) often discuss what students need to know and be able to do in order to lead successful lives. However, we educators must take time to focus on ourselves: what we believe about our roles and our goals as educators. Purkey and Novak (1984) in *Inviting School Success* suggest extending invitations to students in order to make students feel welcome to the educational community. They outline four levels of invitation that impact directly on the academic growth and accomplishments of students. Figure 4.1 outlines the four levels. The levels are also described in the following paragraphs.

Figure 4.1   Purkey's Levels of Inviting

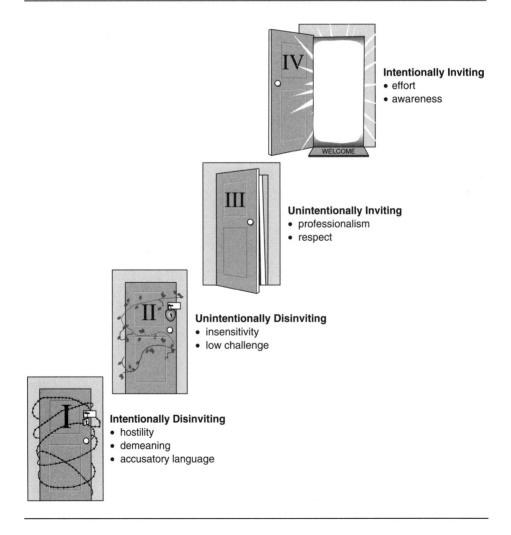

The Will to Succeed

Faith in Human Potential

What are we teachers willing to do to ensure that we have given our all to bring out the best in students? We must be clear about our guiding principles. We must ask ourselves, "What beliefs guide my actions?" Real teaching comes from a deep faith in the human capacity to grow and learn. It emanates from a strong belief in one's purpose and a willingness to express one's convictions in various ways throughout the scope of one's work. Learning involves more than placing a task on the table and saying, "This is what we are going to learn today," and assuming that it will be learned.

"Disinviting" Versus Inviting

Levels 1 and 2—intentionally and unintentionally *"disinviting"*—require students to devise, create, develop, and/or enhance their own skills, talents, self-beliefs, and sheer will to overcome the proverbial beast of defeatism. They must rely on their inner strength to self-motivate. In other words, they must call upon their conative spirit and firmly believe in their own abilities to cope, survive, and succeed emotionally, psychologically, and academically. When the school environment does not invite and welcome students with accommodating, compassionate, and supportive behaviors, actions, and instructional activities, then students must "crash the party" without the benefit of a formal invitation and, with resolve and determination, make themselves welcomed and part of the event. Students must summon conation in its basic form—they must fuel their internal engines so that they can summon the courage, resilience, will, and staying power to "hang in there."

Schools must avoid levels 1 and 2, and should instead invite students to dine at a gourmet buffet that features a variety of intellectual, emotional, and social delicacies. The buffet should nourish students' determination and willpower to confront and overcome any stumbling blocks they may encounter. These delicacies provide students with the aptitudes, attitudes, and abilities they need to undertake life's challenges. Students should be fortified with the determination and the willful power not only to confront, but to overcome, any stumbling blocks they may encounter. Every day schools should initiate, nurture, and provide an innovative, authentic cuisine for the heart and mind of students. Schools must consistently foster students' insatiable appetite for knowledge. While there is no foolproof recipe for alleviating school problems and issues, we can hope, believe, and strive to provide better learning opportunities for students.

TEACHERS MAKE A DIFFERENCE

Teachers are pivotal to student success. While administrators, parents, and other stakeholders play a pertinent role in ensuring that students receive the best educational experiences possible, teachers are the most accountable, because they spend a great deal of contact time with students during the instructional day. Numerous research studies (e.g., Palmer, 1998), professional observations, and interviews indicate the enormous influence and impact that teachers have in tapping their students' potential and bringing out their students' best abilities.

Promoting Conation in the Classroom

If teachers wish to ensure their students' success, they must create conative classrooms. Conative classrooms use life-oriented experiences to create meaning, foster learning, and increase social wellness. Students learn how to make informed decisions and how to become productive citizens. Figure 4.2 illustrates the differences between a conative classroom and a nonconative classroom. The practices that can facilitate learning in the conative domain and strengthen bonds between students and intended goals are shown in Figure 4.3.

Students cannot truly do their best when they are feeling weak, incompetent, or alienated. If we expect learners to produce authentic results, then learners must feel a sense of ownership in their learning. Therefore, it is our job to help students feel strong, capable, and committed. Trust and confidence play a significant role in learning. Without trust and confidence, many students choose not to take risks. Without taking risks, students will not change. Without change, students will not grow.

Teachers seeking to develop their craft to the fullest view conation as a tool, a process, and a measure for gaining insight into when it is best to guide students, when to step back and allow them to move forward on their own, and when to "push" them (Borkowski et al., 1989; Dole et al., 1991; Paris & Winograd, 1990). The conative domain can forge connections between students and the goal, between opportunities and preparation, between inner strength and emotional intelligence, between challenge and stamina, between seeing the bigger picture and working toward that end, between belief in oneself and launching new ideas. Within the conative domain, we learn to give up on giving up; we trade in negative self-talk for breakthrough thinking and living, and we meet challenges with persistence and renewed energy (Gholar et al., 1991).

CONNECTING TO STUDENTS' LIVES OUTSIDE OF SCHOOL

Parents' love and care provide the best start for children in becoming loving and caring people. Simple gestures seem like big celebrations to children. Smiles, hugs, and kind words help to cultivate personal integrity and character. Parents who care enough to take a moment from their busy schedules to play, pause, listen, or simply laugh say to their children, "You

Figure 4.2 Conative Versus Nonconative Classrooms

Characteristics of Conative Classrooms	Characteristics of Nonconative Classrooms
• Students are actively engaged and take ownership of their learning	• Students are disengaged and disinterested in learning.
• Teachers and students share mutual respect and joy.	• Teachers and students don't enjoy being in the classroom together and look forward to the end of the day.
• Collaboration is part of instruction.	• Instructional autonomy is the rule. There's only one way—the teacher's way.
• The classroom is a caring learning community.	• The classroom is a cold, unaccommodating, and uncaring environment.
• independence and interdependence are communicated and experienced daily.	• Independence and interdependence are discouraged. Students are asked to simply do what they are told.
• Learning is appropriately rigorous and always supportive.	• Learning is inappropriately rigorous or lacking structure, substance, standards, or purpose.
• Students know and use the conative power within themselves to make wise choices.	• Students show lackluster performance, make poor choices, and are unfocused and apathetic.
• Students can be seen giving theri best inside and outside the classroom.	• Students can be seen demonstrating inappropriate behavior inside and outside the classroom.
• Students feel and express a genuine sense of belonging.	• Students feel and express a sense of alienation and rejection.
• Teachers know their students and are open and accepting of all learners. They make the classroom an inviting place.	• Teachers are rigid and lack interest in some students' needs while showing favoritism toward others. They make the classroom a "disinviting" place.
• Teachers believe that students have varied strengths and can all strive.	• Teachers believe it is the students' job to pay attention and learn, whether or not teachers provide differentiated learning.
• Students believe in themselves and put forth effort to learn, while their teachers encourage them to establish and maintain personal standars of excellence.	• Students fail to believe in themselves, put forth little effort to learn, and are angry and frustrated, while their teachers fail to encourage them to establish and maintain personal standards of excellence.

are special, and someone special cares for you!" Being an integral part of a child's life gives both the adult and the young person permission to experience life in the moment. Bonds between parent and child that are grounded in a warm, nurturing environment build special relationships. In these relationships it is often difficult to tell who admires the other more. A child's inborn sense of wonder needs the companionship of at least one person who can share it.

Figure 4.3   Teacher Actions That Promote Student Resilience

- **R**ecognize special gifts and talents of students, even if there is no place to show them on the report card.
- **E**mpower students by helping them to succeed in at least one small way each day.
- **S**mile when you see your students.
- **I**f you do not like something a student has done, help the individual understand that you still value him or her as a person.
- **L**isten (be fully present) when your students speak.
- **I**gnite the will to learn by seeking to know students beyond the facade they wear.
- **E**ncourage students to aim high.
- **N**urture excellence by inviting students to experience your excellence.
- **C**all students by their names.
- **E**nlighten students' view of what they can become and they will seek to give to you and the world the best of who they are.

Adults can encourage children to hope and dream by sharing their own hopes and aspirations with children. Parent-child relationships enable children to connect their dreams to self-confident, thoughtful actions. Healthy communication is key to developing a healthy self-image. Children desire to partake of life's fullness when they experience personal interactions that include vision, knowledge, and compassion. Young people of character walk not in your shadow, but in your light.

"The way schools care about children is reflected in the way schools care about student families" (Epstein, 1995, p. 701). Students' families (or other external support systems) are an essential part of a student's success in life and in school. However, engaging families in the learning process can be challenging. When parents have experienced negative situations in their own school careers, they may feel uncomfortable or even combative when they speak with teachers. Try meeting at a neutral location or communicating through telephone calls, notes, or e-mail messages. Share positive news about students and offer constructive, "do-able" strategies that parents can implement to increase students' success (Barr & Parrett, 2003).

ENSURING THE ACADEMIC SUCCESS OF ADOLESCENTS

In 1977, Lispsitz conducted a classic study subtitled *A Review of Research and Programs Concerning Early Adolescence*. This study focused attention on early adolescence—a unique stage of human development. Subsequent studies (McCombs & Whisler, 1989; Sizer, 1984) have indicated that young people between the ages of ten and fifteen face many challenges due to changes in their physical, social, emotional, mental, and moral development. "No other age level is of more importance to the future of individuals, and, literally, to that of society; because these are the years when youngsters crystallize their beliefs about themselves and firm up their self-concepts, their philosophies of life, and their values—the things that are the ultimate determinants of their behavior" (Lounsbury, 1996).

A Parent's Thoughts on Raising Her Middle School Child

When asked to share her thoughts on raising children, a parent I met at a conference said to me, "I'm not giving up on my child. Sometimes I get tired—trying to keep my son on the road to success. Each time I feel like quitting, I remember that in the game of life, we are both situated in the fourth quarter of the game. By virtue of being the mother of an adolescent—the fourth quarter of childhood will soon be ending. Will he wait on the sidelines for my arrival if I'm not there for him? I don't think so. So many voices, good and bad, are knocking at my son's door right now. Which ones will he listen to?

The only time I have is *right now*—to make a difference in his life." Again she said, "I'm not giving up on my child." She went on to tell me, "He loves basketball. I'm present at all of his games and I'm present at his school, not because he is in trouble, that's not an issue for us. I'm there because he is my son. I see him as a leader and I tell him this every day. I believe in him and I know that he believes in himself. As a single mother, I'm his coach, his cheerleader, his disciplinarian and many times, I'm the whole village. Too often no one comes around to encourage or build him up.

In a world where it seems that nothing really matters because everything is allowed, I'm his moral compass and his mentor. We talk, he listens and I listen to him. We talk about what it means to be a man, a good man, a responsible person, a success in life. It's not easy. He's my son. I'm proud of him."

Those of us who interact with adolescents on a regular basis know that many of the perceptions and beliefs attributed to them are generally stereotypical, negative, and even mythical. Figure 4.4: A Profile of Today's Adolescent points out the complex needs and characteristics of today's youth. Some general characteristics that have been ascribed to middle school students include the idea that they are "a composite of raging hormones, who are often confused about who they are, want to be, or should be. They have a difficult time accepting their physical and emotional transformations; often see themselves as unattractive, unaccepted, unappreciated, and even unloved. They want very much to 'fit in,' but frequently feel isolated by their peers, teachers, and family."

In addition to the changes adolescents typically face, some adolescents experience social and emotional trauma, display antisocial behaviors, and exhibit a lack of moral and value-based attitudes and actions. Of course,

Figure 4.4   A Profile of Today's Adolescent

May Be . . .	Yet May . . .
Technologically "Savvy"	Lack skill to organize, evaluate, synthesize data
Multicultural, Multilingual	Feel stymied by the ideas and language of one's culture
Used to Fast Access	Lack motivation to persevere for task completion
Socially Active	Lack the skills for purposeful social interaction
Peer Oriented	Need assistance with interpersonal relationships
Intellectually Capable	Be unpracticed in higher cognitive thinking
Future Oriented	Lack the skills for self-management and regulation
Exposed to Experience	Struggle with moral and ethical decisions
Information-Rich	Be limited in opportunities to explore broader issues
Independent-Minded	Be personally vulnerable to peer and societal lure
College-Work-Bound	Be limited in practical knowledge

From *Teaching with Adolescent Learning in Mind* by Glenda Ward Beamon, 2001, Thousand Oaks, CA: Corwin Press. Reprinted with permission.

we know these characteristics do not apply to all adolescents; however, research demonstrates that this population is at risk for succumbing to these negative characteristics.

Most young adolescents are quite "normal," according to research data and personal observations. They have strong morals and core values that preclude their participation in premarital sex, indulgence in alcohol and drugs, or other unacceptable social behaviors. They travel down the road of puberty rather effortlessly, avoiding many of the ditches of despair and potholes of uncertainty and confusion about their self-identity and future. They are happy, humorous, trusting, adventuresome, clever, smart, street-wise, challenging, and hopeful. According to Piaget (as cited in Gunning, 2000), young adolescents are also able to think abstractly and to reason hypothetically. (Piaget called this the formal-operational stage of cognitive development, which typically occurs between the ages of eleven and fifteen.)

Dream Big!

Our challenge is to explore ways to strengthen light in the midst of shadow. We must build connections in order to promote positive changes in behavior. We must use practical strategies that lead to excellence in school, at home, in the community, and throughout life. Through the passion of the will, we pursue excellence. Through the pursuit of excellence we climb—lifting others, setting them free to live, hope, and find themselves. Together we learn to run with our dreams.

Addressing Feelings of Isolation and Hopelessness

Too many students feel like they are outsiders at school. Unfortunately, these feelings of alienation and isolation often increase as students get older. The poem "I Wish You Could Feel My Rage!" vividly illustrates one high school student's feelings of alienation.

I Wish You Could Feel My Rage!

Oh how I wish you could feel my rage!
I breathe in deeply, close my eyes, in darkness I exhale and ask . . .
Why do I have this rage within me?

The pain . . .
It comes on slowly and fiercely explodes into a fiery tidal wave
of contention.

If only you knew how it feels to be an outcast among peers
for no reason . . .
No future ahead—and nothing behind.

The emptiness, the loneliness
Wanting to be a part of something more
Rejected . . .

Made to feel useless—no purpose for living
Entombed and dead before I die
I wish you could feel my rage!

Young people who see themselves as losers create their own sense of truth. Have students work through the instructional activity "Anger: Thinking it Through," to help them mitigate feelings of anger and hopelessness. When teachers and schools work together with parents and other caregivers to support students, their attitudes, and thus their academic achievement and conative spirit, can change for the better.

MODELS OF PERSEVERANCE

As early as preschool, children hear the fable of the tortoise and the hare and discover that the slow tortoise persevered to beat the hare in a seemingly impossible race. They also marvel at *The Little Engine That Could* (Piper, 1991). Each time the train engine says, "I think I can, I think I can," it puts forth more effort into climbing the mountain and it eventually succeeds! Children also watch and cheer *The Lion King* (Allers et al., 1994) and similar movies that portray courage, convictions, and the belief in one's self and one's ability.

The Will to Succeed

Through a Child's Eyes

Children help us escape from the busyness of our day-to-day routines, to enter a place called "right here, and right now." They are experts at living in the moment. Step into their world. Share moments of joy watching each other celebrate your lives!

As students grow, they begin to read about real people such as the Wright brothers, Harriet Tubman, Helen Keller, Jackie Robinson, and Anne Frank. Through *The Wright Brothers: How They Invented the Airplane* (Freeman, 1991), students learn that even though many others had failed and even died trying to attempt to fly, the Wright brothers were not deterred from their quest to fly. They experienced failure in their early attempts, but did not give up. They were self-motivated, had the will to succeed, and continuously put forth the effort needed to succeed in getting a plane to fly.

When students read about Harriet Tubman, they discover another person who had conation. She was determined to lead as many slaves as possible to freedom. Even the threat of capture or death did not deter her will or impede her efforts to succeed in her mission. Students are engrossed with *The Story of My Life* (Keller, 2003) because they are fascinated with Helen Keller's drive, will, determination, and successful struggle to surmount what many would consider insurmountable obstacles. Stories about Jackie Robinson (e.g., *Jackie Robinson: Pro Ball's First Black Star* [Olsen, 1974]) also captivate students' attention as they discover how he fought discrimination and extreme racial prejudices to become America's first black major league baseball player. Jackie Robinson's story is yet another stellar example of pure drive, will, courage, and determination that inspires students of all ethnic and cultural heritages.

In *Anne Frank: The Diary of a Young Girl* (1956), students find themselves vicariously enduring the fear and ordeals faced by Anne, her family, and her friends. They also come to admire these people's tenacious will to survive and live in the midst of such cognitive dissonance. The life stories of people such as Winston Churchill, Tecumseh, Dr. Severo Ochoa, Cesar Chavez, and Nelson Mandela are other examples of individuals who persevered by sheer will, determination, and effort.

CONATION MOVES THE HEART OF A TEACHER

It is within each teacher's power to help students face challenge, and defeat the shadows of uncertainty, apathy and hopelessness. I am reminded of Victor, one of my eighth-grade students, age sixteen, diagnosed as a nonreader. Victor had been "socially promoted" throughout

> ## The Will to Succeed
>
> ### *Lessons Learned in Light and Shadow*
> The events of childhood linger long after the wonder and wisdom are gone. Lessons learned in shadow and in light often repeat themselves in the generations that follow. Our relationships with children affect the character and resilience of these children and of future generations. Through teaching, we not only affect the children before us, but we also influence our nation's intellectual, economic, social, and ethical future. How will the experiences of our students impact on what they will become? What will their experiences say about who we are? Are we instilling in them the fundamental core knowledge, beliefs, and values from which they can build their lives? What are we giving them to build upon? Stop, look, and listen to the lives of children.

his elementary school tenure. Once again he was repeating the process of doing nothing but waiting for time to pass in order to move from one grade to the next. He knew that due to his age, he would be in high school next year. Therefore, very little sparked his interest or motivation to learn. Unfortunately, he was just one of many in this particular class who were lost in the shadows of defeat and hopelessness.

I had a ritual of reading to my students every afternoon, immediately after lunch for approximately ten minutes. My strategy for doing this was simply to motivate these students; to try to rekindle that flame of curiosity and the desire to learn; and to chase away the shadows of disinterest, lack of confidence, frustration, and lost hope. I also wanted to motivate their interest in reading novels. I chose the novel *Bury My Heart at Wounded Knee: An Indian History of the American West*, written by Dee Brown. Each day, I would pre-select an exciting section at which to stop. Every day, I noticed more and more of my students, all of whom were African Americans, including of course Victor, rushing into the room, getting quiet and admonishing peers to settle down in order that I might continue the saga of *Wounded Knee*.

One day after reading part of the chapter I had chosen for the afternoon, I closed the book, much to the groaning and pleading of several students to please just read a little bit more. Later, Victor quietly came to me and asked in a whispered voice, "Can I borrow your book and take it home, just for tonight? I promise I will bring it back in the morning, but I have just got to find out what happened to Little Crow and his warriors when they went to get food from the soldiers, and you are reading too slow. I am going to ask my brother to read it to me so I can find out what happened. I don't want to have to wait for you to get to it tomorrow. I want to know today!"

Of course I let Victor borrow the book. He took it home, and as promised, returned it the next day, with a "smug smile" and the knowledge that he knew something no one else in the class knew or would know until I read to them after lunch.

But after that incident, I also noticed Victor as he began asking classmates questions about what this or that word was. He actually started taking "easy reading books" out of the library. The light of knowledge inspired Victor to ask questions and begin to try. The adage, "Better late than never" came to mind, as I watched, helped, and shared Victor's frustrations to overcome eight years of "nonlearning." I also shared in Victor's joy when he read two lines of a beginning-to-read book all by himself. This was the joy of triumph over defeat. This was Victor's very first step into the world of conation, a learning domain that gave him the energy and the will to strive, and not give up.

Success, through positive self-direction, was new for Victor. The experience of "light winning over darkness" was a new beginning for Victor, just as important as learning to read those two lines. If I did no more than play a role in freeing Victor from his own self-doubt, my success was in liberating his thinking about who he was and his potential to do more, and become more than what he had previously allowed himself to do and become.

Unfortunately, Victor dropped out of high school after the first month of his freshman year. Is he a failure? I cannot answer that question. As a teacher, I can confidently say that I reached within the conative domain and nurtured seeds that had been planted and actually took root right before my eyes. I will always remember the triumphant smile and look of accomplishment on his face as he struggled from within to learn how to read, not for me, but for himself. For that brief moment, light had chased the shadows and won.

I lost track of Victor, and often wonder if that small step into the world of learning expanded his capacity to understand that success is truly an "inside job." I wonder if he understood that victory is triumph over challenge. He indeed was the victor.

Stretching the boundaries of possibilities involves shattering old conventions.

Energies devoted to finding new ways to address issues in education opens opportunities for reaching the heart of learning, namely, issues facing the human side of the curriculum. One's beliefs, and perception of reality, can impact the outcomes of teaching and learning. It is important to keep in mind that shadows and transformations can be birthed into life, or become stillborn, due to a lack of nurturing on the human side of the curriculum. The human side of the curriculum drives the performance side. In helping students confront the reality of who they are, we must help them explore what they believe about themselves.

The lessons at the end of this chapter acquaint students with stories of perseverance. The lessons motivate students to establish and reach for their own goals so that they might better understand the concept of conation.

THE ORIGINS OF SUCCESS AND FAILURE

Our nation needs productive students and resilient teachers who are prepared and committed to give their personal and professional best. Meeting the needs of *all* learners involves instructional leadership—leadership that transforms and differentiates instruction in order to increase academic achievement. The conative domain provides an access route for building greater collaboration and deeper engagement in the process of learning. Teachers can foster the underlying thinking needed to positively influence students' academic and social behavior, while laying the groundwork that ensures that students are interested in what they are being taught.

Teachers who focus on conation also seek to enhance students' problem-solving and question-posing skills. In this process, the teacher's role becomes more and more transparent. That is, the teacher refrains from *delivering* lessons and instead shifts to *mentoring* students in finding and solving problems. In this role, the teacher becomes aware of the conative power of teachable moments. Teachable moments take students beyond the immediate lesson, drawing them into asking significant how and why questions (e.g., "How can I accomplish this?" and "Why is it important for me to learn this?"). Excellent teachers have the courage to extend themselves in order to bridge the gap between emerging understanding and complete understanding. When we keep conation in mind, we strengthen teacher-student relationships through consensus-building and support. As we become better mentors, students build self-knowledge, mental toughness, emotional resilience, and personal commitment.

We educators often hear the statement, "Start where they are." When we begin with conation in mind, we discover that students may not "start" where first anticipated. Some may be more advanced; others may need additional support. Some students may require a stronger and more positive union between self-perception and their willingness to try. Remember, schools serve students with tremendously diverse backgrounds and personal beliefs about learning. We must be prepared to provide students with multiple entry and exit points in the learning process. For example, we should:

- acknowledge each student's growth and achievement, while maintaining focus on curriculum and instruction;
- support and encourage students to open themselves to learning without restrictions and to fully engage in the learning process; and
- hold high expectations for all learners, even those who appear to struggle or who are reluctant to learn.

If we keep conation in mind, we will know when to lead, when to gently push students, and when to let go, allowing learners to soar in varied and unique ways with their academic pursuits.

Lessons From the Heart of Learning

We often hear the statement, "If we don't learn from history, we are doomed or bound to repeat it." This concept is lost on too many of our young people because they live and learn just for the present. There is a great deal to be learned from real and fictional events about ethical behavior, treatment of our fellow man, our individual values and beliefs, and the crucial role of the will in the struggle for survival, existence, and "the good life."

The following lessons have been designed to motivate students' interest in and knowledge of events in history, as well as fictional accounts, that have inspired some individuals to willfully perform feats of unselfishness, bravery, and compassion; or events that provoked others to use their gift of determination and perseverance to engage in undesirable and detrimental activities. These lessons challenge students to reflect on their actions, motives, beliefs, values, and hopefully, gain a better understanding of ethical behavior.

AM I MY BROTHER'S KEEPER?

I expect to pass through life but once. If therefore, there be any kindness I can show, or any good thing I can do to any fellow human being, let me do it now, and not defer or neglect it, as I shall not pass this way again.

—William Penn, 1644

WHAT'S IT ALL ABOUT?

Grade Level: Middle and High School

Purpose

- To acquaint students with historical events that impacted millions of lives
- To promote a better understanding of discrimination and intolerance
- To help students discover how one person's courageous voice, actions, and care can make a difference
- To help students understand that "people are people" regardless of culture, religion, or ethnicity
- To have students recognize that all human life has value and worth

Instructional Objectives

- Students will develop an appreciation for and understanding of historical events.
- Students will improve their comprehension and critical thinking skills.
- Students will enhance their knowledge and understanding of characterization in nonfiction genres.
- Students will explore the concept of "man's inhumanity to man."
- Students will explore cognitive, affective, and conative behaviors via various historical events.
- Students will examine the power of metaconation in ethical decision making.

Interdisciplinary Implementation

- History
- Language arts
- Library science
- Career education
- Technology

Instructional Focus

Students will read "Stranger on the Bus" and reflect on the following:

- research methodology;
- reading, writing, and thinking; and
- metacognition.

MAKING THE CONNECTION

Instructional Strategies and Activities

1. Encourage students to read "Stranger on the Bus."
2. Divide students into cooperative groups of three to five students.
3. Ask students to answer the following questions (in their groups or as a whole class):
   - Why do you think the man came to the rescue of the Jewish woman?
   - Why do you think he risked his life to help this woman?
   - Would you consider him courageous, brave, and sympathetic? Give reasons and examples for your response.
   - Do you think you would have or could have acted in the same manner had you been this man? Why or why not?
   - What kind of person would he have to be to do what he did?
   - Why do you think there was so much hatred for Jews?
   - Why do you think there is still hatred, resentment, and discrimination against certain ethnic groups in this, the twenty-first century?
4. Discuss students' answers to the questions. Use students' answers to motivate them to complete the research project (see Extended Research).

CONATIVE INSIGHT: Now that I *know*, what will I do?

Extended Research and Reflection

1. Challenge teams to conduct research about this period of history. Explain that they should use historical texts, the Internet, and other resources to learn about and acquaint themselves with this period. Tell students to read historical stories (e.g., *Anne Frank: Diary of a Young Girl*) or watch movies (e.g., *Schindler's List, The Pianist*) that depict the horrors of the Holocaust.

2. Ask students to examine, discuss, and note significant events such as the rise of Hitler, the growing resentment of and discrimination toward the Jewish population, the establishment of the death camps, etc.

3. Challenge each team to select one or more of these events to research. Explain that the team should compile its findings by writing a collective research paper.

4. Encourage teams to share their papers with the class.

Stranger on the Bus

by Lawrence Kushner

A light snow was falling and the streets were crowded with people. It was Munich in Nazi Germany. One of my rabbinic students, Shifra Penzias, told me her great-aunt, Sussie, had been riding a city bus home from work when SS storm troopers suddenly stopped the coach and began examining the identification papers of the passengers. Most were annoyed but a few were terrified. Jews were being told to leave the bus and get into a truck around the corner.

My student's great-aunt watched from her seat in the rear as the soldiers systematically worked their way down the aisle. She began to tremble, tears streaming down her face. When the man next to her noticed she was crying, he politely asked her why.

"I don't have the papers you have. I am a Jew. They're going to take me."

The man exploded with disgust. He began to curse and scream at her. "You stupid [woman]," he roared. "I can't stand being near you!"

The SS men asked what all the yelling was about.

"Damn her," the man shouted angrily. "My wife has forgotten her papers again! I'm so fed up. She always does this!"

The soldiers laughed and moved on.

My student said that her great-aunt never saw the man again. She never even knew his name.

Excerpt from Invisible Lines of Connection: Sacred Stories of the Ordinary. © 1996 Lawrence Kushner (Woodstock, VT: Jewish Lights Publishing). Permission granted by Jewish Lights Publishing, P.O. Box 237, Woodstock, VT 05091 http://www.jewishlights.com.

Ask students to reflect upon the following questions:

- Have you acquired a better understanding of this period in history? What have you learned?
- Have you heard of, read about, or watched movies that depict the cruelty of humans against fellow humans (man's inhumanity to man)? For example, have you heard about the poor treatment of Chinese people, the cruelties of slavery, and the interment of Japanese Americans?
- Have any of your previous concepts, biases, or misconceptions about certain cultures or ethnic groups changed? (Note: If students feel uncomfortable, they need not answer this question aloud. Rather, encourage them to reflect on the question privately.)

ASSESSMENT

Assess the success of the lesson by asking yourself the following questions:

1. Did students gain a new body of knowledge about historical events or events that included discrimination and prejudice? How did they demonstrate this knowledge?
2. How effectively did students apply their metacognitive, literacy, and critical thinking skills? How was this evidenced?
3. Were students able to understand the underlying theme (how individuals and groups are able to persevere and survive under impossible odds and conditions)? How was this evidenced by each student?

DOES THE END JUSTIFY THE MEANS?

What lies behind us and what lies before us are tiny matters compared to what lies within us.

—Ralph Waldo Emerson

WHAT'S IT ALL ABOUT?

Grade Level: Elementary, Middle, and High School

Purpose

- To acquaint students with the elements of fictional stories
- To develop an awareness of ethical values and positive character traits
- To promote an understanding of intrinsic motivation
- To emphasize the importance of moral decisions
- To help students understand the power of the will

Instructional Objectives

- Students will develop an understanding of caring, responsibility, honesty, and courage and how these traits impact one's life.
- Students will develop a knowledge and understanding of narrative, expository, descriptive, and persuasive writing.
- Students will explore their creative writing abilities.
- Students will enhance their inference, critical thinking, and comprehension skills.
- Students will examine moral issues and will discuss whether or not particular situations justify illegal actions.

Interdisciplinary Implementation

- Assessment
- Language arts
- Library science
- Science
- Character education

Instructional Focus

Have your students read "The Story of Jack and the Beanstalk." They will:

- Be able to relate fiction with real life incidents in determining values
- Be able to recognize and determine ethical issues dealing with right vs. wrong
- Be able to use fictional narrative to develop and/or enhance skills in creative writing, inferring, comprehending, and distinguishing the various writing discourses

MAKING THE CONNECTION

Instructional Strategies and Activities

Part 1: Writing Activities

1. Divide students into cooperative teams of three to five students. Ask teams to read the retold version of "Jack and the Beanstalk."
2. Challenge teams to complete the writing activities at the end of the story.
3. Encourage teams to share their writing with the other teams. Discuss the presentations. Then compare the presentations and select the most original and creative responses.

Part 2: Jack—A Hero or a Criminal?

4. Place students in three cooperative teams for a debate. Explain each team's role:

   a. **Team A** will take the pro position: Jack was justified in going into the giant's castle, taking advantage of his unhappy wife, and stealing his possessions. This team will argue the case that Jack had conative qualities, that he was brave, strong-minded, and persistent in his endeavors to provide for his mother and himself. Team A will also argue that the giant's death was accidental and he deserved to die. Team A will be in favor of declaring Jack a hero, who exhibited bravery, tenacity, and responsibility for his actions.

   b. **Team B** will take the con position (the opposite position from Team A): Jack was a common thief and murderer, in spite of his dire circumstances. It will contend that Jack was not an acceptable role model for exhibiting perseverance or determination just because he continued to return to the castle in spite of the danger of being discovered. This team will be opposed to attributing any positive characteristics to Jack or his actions. Jack will be portrayed as dishonest, conniving, lazy, and a murderous thief. This team will address the ethical dilemma of Jack's behavior as an example of metaconation. Did his actions "justify the means?"

   c. **Team C** will act as a panel of adjudicators. Members of this team will listen to the rationale, arguments, and justifications presented by Team A and Team B, and then determine which team best supported its pro or con position. Team C may use the Debate Scoring Sheet to record points earned by Team A and Team B.

5. Hold the debate. Team C will determine which team presented the most convincing presentation relating to ethical behavior.

Jack—A Hero or a Criminal?
Rubric for Evaluating Debate

Directions: Determine the number of points each team earns on each of the skills listed below. Check the appropriate numerical box using the key guide. Total the ten features. Highest possible points = 50.

Key: 5 = Exceptionally effective; 4 = Highly effective; 3 = Proficiently effective; 2 = Slightly effective; 1 = Absolutely ineffective

Presentation/Organization	Team A					Team B				
	5	4	3	2	1	5	4	3	2	1
1. Spoke clearly, used correct sentence structure and appropriate, fluent, and creative vocabulary										
2. Used effective verbal and nonverbal communication (voice quality, body language, eye contact)										
3. Answered questions with details and examples										
4. Addressed the issue effectively, to the point, and in a sincere manner										
5. Exhibited respect and demonstrated appreciation for others' viewpoints										
6. Presented viewpoints in an organized and logical manner										
7. Provided justification for answers, comments, and conclusions										
8. Maintained focus on the topic; delivery of ideas connected logically										
9. Presented characters, their values, beliefs, attributes, character traits, and personalities in an inspired, creative, and thought-provoking manner										
10. Convinced jury (Team C) of the validity of points of view presented; persuaded and won the sentiment and votes of this panel										

Total for Team A: _____   Total for Team B: _____

CONATIVE INSIGHT: Now that I *know*, what will I do?

Extended Research and Reflection

Encourage students to consider how they might have handled:

- selling the cow?
- making (or not making) trips up the beanstalk?
- the incident with the giant?

Extended Writing & Critical Thinking Activities

1. You are a reporter for your local newspaper and you have been given the assignment of interviewing the giant's wife after the giant's death. Create five significant questions you will ask her as you attempt to discover what really happened. Imagine how she might answer the questions and write about her version of the incident. (Narrative)

2. Using your prior knowledge about plants and their growth cycle, create a fictional bean and a scientific explanation for the type of beans Jack obtained from the stranger. Base your explanation on real scientific facts about plants. (Expository)

3. Jack was eventually caught and charged with breaking, entering, and murder. You are his attorney. You must convince the jury that Jack is innocent of all charges. You must gather evidence (create this evidence), interview witnesses (make up interviews), and write your findings for presentation to the jury. How will you convince the jury that what Jack did was not wrong and that he is innocent? (Persuasive)

4. In your summation (as Jack's lawyer), one strategy you will use is to create as much sympathy and empathy for your client as possible. Therefore, you must paint a graphic picture, with explicit and descriptive details and examples about Jack's environment (e.g., his single-parent home, his neighborhood, his mother's lack of parenting skills, etc.). Create a description that will bring the jurors to tears. (Descriptive and Creative)

ASSESSMENT

Assess the success of the lesson by asking yourself the following questions:

1. Did students exhibit a knowledge of conventional writing skills and the writing process? How?
2. How did students demonstrate their understanding of fictional characters and fictional incidents in the story?
3. Were students able to identify and understand the underlying themes of responsibility, dishonesty, bravery, and determination? How was this demonstrated by each student?
4. Do students know and understand the tenets of narrative, expository, persuasive, and descriptive writing? How did students exhibit this knowledge and understanding?
5. Were students able to understand the difference between ethical and unethical actions? How was this demonstrated?

The Story of Jack and the Beanstalk

Retold by Ernestine Riggs

Once upon a time there lived, in a very poor town, a boy named Jack and his mother. Now Jack was not the brightest boy, but he had a good disposition, told great jokes, and was kind and loving. He was, however, extremely lazy. Some attributed his laziness to the fact that he just was not "self-motivated!" Jack's mother, like most mothers, loved her son, but knew he had a few cards missing from the deck when it came to him using his most capable brain.

One day, after the mother had given Jack the last piece of bread in the house, she looked around and realized she had sold every possible possession they had in the world in her effort to feed herself and her son. All they had left of any value was the old, dried-out cow. So she gave Jack the responsibility of taking their last food source to town to sell.

She explained to Jack the importance of getting the highest possible price for the cow. The more money he was able to get, the more food they could buy, and the longer they would be able to survive.

Happy that his mother trusted him with this significant task, Jack set off for town with the old cow. He had not gotten very far before he encountered a strange looking little individual who, after talking to Jack for a few minutes, knew Jack was an easy mark. He talked Jack into trading the cow for five pretty beans. Jack ran home, proud and excited, thinking he had made a great deal. Of course you know what his mother thought! She was so angry that she threw the beans out of the window, where they landed in the back yard. She sent Jack to bed hungry.

Well, the next day when Jack woke up, to his great surprise, he found a gigantic beanstalk had grown from the beans his mother had thrown out of the window. Like most boys he was curious, so he climbed up the beanstalk and stepped into a strange and different land. After checking out his surroundings, he spied a castle down the road. He approached the castle cautiously, walked up to the huge doors, knocked timidly, and asked for some food.

It so happened the castle belonged to a "cannibal giant." Luckily for Jack, the giant's wife came to the door. She informed him of the giant's fondness for "people stew" and begged him to leave. But Jack sweet-talked her into letting him in the house, whereby she fed him a delicious vegetarian meal.

Now the giant's wife had been married, as far as she was concerned, much too long. In fact, she was really tired of the bulky, repulsive, gluttonous giant and longed to be free and single again. When the giant returned home unexpectedly early, she hid Jack in the oven where he remained until the giant fell asleep. When Jack was sure the giant was sleeping soundly, he stole the hen that produced golden eggs and ran home via the beanstalk.

He and his mother lived quite well until the hen ceased laying the golden eggs. This turn of events created the need for another trip up the beanstalk.

Jack again convinced the wife to allow him entrance into the castle, where he proceeded to rummage around until he found a golden harp. However, when he attempted its theft, it played a "help me" song which woke the giant, causing Jack to run for his life. The giant tried to follow Jack down the beanstalk, but Jack managed to get down first, grab an ax, and chop down the stalk with the giant swaying on it. Needless to say, the big guy was killed.

Jack and his mother, concerned about the legal consequences of the incident, went to the town's psychic, who assured them they would live rich and happy lives forever and ever.

ANGER: THINKING IT THROUGH

When Hurt People . . . Hurt People, No One Wins
—Gholar and Riggs

WHAT'S IT ALL ABOUT?

Grade Level: Elementary, Middle, and High School

Purpose

- To develop an awareness of "uncontrollable rage" in oneself
- To help students understand the difference between anger and rage
- To help students develop skills and strategies that will help them recognize their anger
- To help students minimize their episodes of rage
- To make students aware that they are in control of and responsible for their emotional actions

Instructional Objectives

- Students will develop a knowledge base of such terms as mad, anger, rage, furious, boiling mad, seething, ire, and similar others.
- Students will be able to define and discuss the level of intensity of these terms.
- Students will discuss and develop personal strategies as to how to control their anger and rage.
- Students will think of ways to use their conative spirit to help them control their tempers and emotional outbursts.

Interdisciplinary Implementation

- Language arts
- History
- Character education
- Sociology
- Psychology
- Self-reflection and assessment

MAKING THE CONNECTION

Instructional Strategies and Activities

A Cup of Wisdom . . .

Never allow anger to trap you into negative or limited thinking about who you are and what you can become. Let the greatness in you set you apart from giving into what could escalate into an emotional disaster. Your best is not somewhere *out there*, it is in you.

Actions motivated solely by anger can leave lasting personal scars long after the situation or event you face is over. When you are upset with someone or something, ask yourself: "What is the best thing that I can do with the anger I feel right now?" Ask someone that you trust if there are other ways to resolve a specific personal conflict.

Think about this quote:

Do not do to others that which would anger you if others did it to you.

—Isocrates

Rewrite this quote in your own words. Write an example of what this means.

_____

_____

_____

_____

_____

_____

_____

_____

_____

_____

CONATIVE INSIGHT: Now that I *know*, what will I do?

Extended Research and Reflection

Did You Know . . . ?

Some will find the idea of thinking first before reacting is an easy task. Others will find it more challenging. However, one thing for certain is when you pay attention to your life and prepare yourself to make wise decisions, you will find that you are in charge. You are in control of a wide range of ways to deal with difficult problems as well as ways to resolve your anger. You will be able to move beyond your frustrations in a manner that you can be proud of *today*, and when you look back on *yesterday*, you will still be proud *tomorrow*.

A soft answer turneth away wrath.

—Proverbs

What do you think this wise saying means?

_____

_____

_____

_____

Something to Think About . . .

Responding to situations that strike anger in our hearts involves more than giving into our emotions. Our best responses involve thinking and then making the best choices.

Anger in and of itself may not be all bad. Did you know that anger can actually make us wake up and pay attention to who we are and the power within us to make a difference? When we step away from anger, we can clear our minds and see what is important and what is not.

One question you will come face-to-face with at various times in your life will be the question of character. Over a lifetime, how we choose to deal with anger will tell us a lot about our character. You see, your character is simply who you are, even when no one else is around. There will be times when you will probably become angry, and no one else will be around. What will you do? As you continue to build your character, you will discover that anger is an emotion you will be able to effectively deal with . . . as long as you strive to do what is right.

If someone tries to belittle you with unkind words, you know that you are bigger and better than the smallness of their thinking and the rudeness of their vocabulary. No one can define you or diminish the wonderful qualities that belong to you, unless you let them.

Think of a time when you responded to an angry person or reacted to a potentially explosive situation with "soft words." Describe this situation. Address the following questions to help in your description.

- Who or what was the person/event?
- What was the issue or problem?
- What were the *soft words* you used?
- How did the other person react?
- How did you avoid a possible confrontation?
- How did you feel afterwards?

_____

_____

_____

_____

_____

_____

_____

_____

_____

_____

_____

Interpret each of the following phrases and give an example of each:

Don't cut off your nose to spite your face.

_____

_____

_____

_____

Nothing comes of nothing.

_____

_____

_____

_____

When digging a ditch for your enemy, dig two.

_____

_____

_____

_____

When angry, count ten before you speak; if very angry, a hundred.

_____

_____

_____

_____

Read the following similes and metaphors and give your interpretation of their meanings.

Mad as a cat on a hot tin roof.

_____

_____

_____

_____

Anger is the pit of a cherry.

_____

_____

_____

_____

Create two similes and two metaphors of your own that would demonstrate why anger is a negative action or reaction.

_____

_____

_____

_____

_____

_____

_____

_____

_____

_____

ASSESSMENT

Choices, Choices, Choices. What Will You Do?

So, what will you do when anger boils up from deep inside of you? Anger has the potential to bring out the best or worst in each of us. What will you choose?

How will you know that you made the right choice? Well, after your emotions are no longer smoldering, thoughtfully reflect on your decision and actions. Was your decision a responsible one? Did it lead to the best possible outcome? If it did, you made the right choice!

Think of five things you can do, when angry, to help you control your feelings and emotions.

_____

_____

_____

_____

_____

Reflections

Can you do better? Certainly, there is always room to expand your thinking and bring more of the best into your life.

Anger, used, does not destroy. Hatred does."

      —Audre Lorde, "Eye to Eye." Sister Outsider (1984)

Think of ways you can enrich your life and make each day work for you.

_____

_____

_____

_____

_____

First Thoughts—Last Thoughts

When Hurt People . . . Hurt People, No One Wins!

—Gholar and Riggs

What do you think this statement means?

_____

_____

_____

_____

_____

5

For All of Them, I Teach

Reflecting on Your Teaching Philosophy

It's difficult to allow yourself to fail—when you know there are so many people reaching out to help you.

—Tenth-grade student

In teaching, it is impossible to hide behind a mask or label. Working with children lends itself to introspection and self-analysis. I know that this by-product of teaching keeps me coming back year after year even after I swear I'm going to quit!

—Elementary teacher

AUTHENTIC TEACHING IN THE CONATIVE DOMAIN

Authentic teaching is teaching at its best. Authentic teachers use the conative domain to ignite each student's desire to achieve and excel. Authentic teachers create challenging and supportive learning environments in which students engage in significant learning tasks. Teachers and learners understand that learning has intrinsic meaning; they know that learning for the sake of learning is as important as learning the required content. Authentic teachers use sound strategies that foster students' desire to learn. Because students learn to take responsibility for their own learning, teachers need not dominate and control their students, but instead they can lead and facilitate students' learning. Students are inspired to take on difficult and exciting challenges, and teachers build a learning culture that supports the growth of all students.

The Will to Succeed

Two Small Words

To teach: These two small words represent an ongoing and tremendous task. What does it mean to teach? Sometimes it means that a child gains a hero, an educator transforms a life, the human condition is altered, the world is enlightened, and a soul is touched. Sometimes it is a rare and amazing process that simply stretches beyond words.

Find Heroic Ways to Reach All Students

Heroic teachers ask: What inspires the will to teach? What do we hope our students will learn? What have they learned from us so far? Will they learn to believe in themselves and the learning process by how we live together and how we live apart? What will they do with what they know? Hopefully, they will use everything we teach them to better themselves and the world

Authentic teaching is not complete without *caring*. Teachers must reach beyond themselves to ensure that what they teach students connects with their everyday lives. Caring is part of the teaching profession; we cannot put a price tag on it. Caring comes from knowing oneself and one's values. In *The Courage to Teach,* Palmer (1998) explains that teachers must know their "inner terrain"—they must understand themselves. "Good teaching requires self-knowledge: it is a secret hidden in plain sight" (p. 3).

Teaching in the conative domain begins when students walk into the classroom and encounter positive, caring energy. Conative teaching is teaching that cares. It is teaching that questions, seeks in-depth answers, and fosters significant learning.

Remember, students give back what they receive. If we model caring, believing, listening, understanding, and cooperating, students will imitate us. If we work together toward common goals, share ideas, model expected behavior, and mentor, students will want to learn. When we demonstrate a strong will to teach and learn, students achieve higher levels of being, knowing, and acting.

To teach means to have the courage to develop spiritual will—to foster students' inner strength and desire to learn. To teach means to have the courage to foster cultural will—to celebrate the uniqueness of every human who has lived in the past, is living in the present, and will live in the future. To teach means to have the courage to view life as opportunity—to support and transform the human condition. To teach means to have the courage to know ourselves—to invite our unknown, creative, and spiritual components to lead us into responsible action.

USING DIVERSE TEACHING STYLES

Current theory suggests that different teaching situations require different teaching styles (Bellanca, 1990; Bonwell & Eison, 1991; Grasha, 1996; McKeachie, 1986). Students do not learn in the same manner as they did in the era of the one-room schoolhouse. Students are no longer expected to "sit and get"—to remain quiet while the teacher imparts knowledge using the same methodology for all students. Students are much more sophisticated now than they were before the explosion of technology. Research shows that today's students pursue, perceive, and process information differently than did students a decade ago (Dunn & Dunn, 1978; Griggs, 1991; Kolb, 1984; Woods, 1994). Students have different learning styles. Therefore, teachers must use different teaching styles (including various instructional strategies, resources, and technology) to reach them.

The most successful teachers are able to adapt their teaching style to the unique and diverse skills and abilities of their students. A national task force sponsored by the National Association of Secondary School Principals developed this definition of learning styles: "The composite of characteristic cognitive, . . . affective, and physiological factors that serve as relatively stable indicators of how a learner perceives, interacts with, and responds to the learning environment" (Keefe, 1979).

If teachers wish to reach students with different learning styles, they must use teaching strategies and activities that are

- differentiated;
- student-centered;
- goal-oriented;
- spirited;
- considerate;
- reflective;
- direct;
- individual and cooperative;
- inclusive;
- culturally, emotionally, and physically sensitive; and
- engaging and inviting.

Two of the most significant contributions a teacher can make in a classroom are *caring* and *time.* Caring doesn't come wrapped in dollar bills, but the compensation for caring goes beyond what any academic test can measure. Time is something we all have while we have it. It is up to us to choose how we will use it. Those who have the will to teach all students give their students time and caring. They are sensitive to their students' needs.

Giving of yourself for a cause or an interest is an honorable way to share and invite others into your life. Teachers who have the will to teach give time and caring to reach the goal of authentic student success. Unfortunately, some teachers fail to appreciate students as individuals and are not interested in moving outside the rote domain of teaching and testing. Instead, they focus on high performance. Although high performance is a worthy goal, teachers must also instill in students a sense of meaning, fairness, belonging, hope, and empowerment to effect change. One of the best indicators that courageous teaching is taking place in a classroom is that morale is high and students are interested in learning, often even excited about learning! Teachers are paying attention to students in these classrooms. For many young people, this "paying attention" is affirming, as evidenced by the following student voices:

> *Being able to ask questions and get answers or clues is helpful to me in school. In reading, I'm successful because I have a partner to read with. We help each other read smoothly and correctly. If we are unsure of what to do, our teacher guides us. Being able to have a partner motivates me to get A's.*
>
> —Fourth-grade student

> *At my school, teachers take time with you and they make it seem like they really like you and care about you. Maybe it's because I listen.*
>
> —Fourth-grade student

The Will to Succeed

Acts of Courage

The conative connection transforms dreams into reality, pain into triumph, defeat into success, frustration into joy, low test scores into high test scores, low achievement into high performance, success into significance. The conative connection builds positive attitudes and productive relationships, transforms bias into open-minded objectivity, and changes negative self-fulfilling prophecies into positive acts of courage.

A reporter once asked Winston Churchill to share his secret to success. He replied, "I can tell you that in just seven words: Never give up, never ever give up!"

THE CHOICE TO TEACH

When we choose to teach, we also acknowledge that we not only choose to learn about our subject matter, but we also choose to learn about those who journey with us—students, parents, and fellow educators. We seek to understand how students see themselves and how they see the world around them (their world view). The principles of conation maintain that students can be taught that they have the power to choose to learn and to lead positive and productive lives. We must take time to help students make conative connections.

Lecturing doesn't change behavior; teaching that addresses diverse learning styles, demonstrates caring, and fosters conation changes behavior. Teachers who listen, understand, provide wisdom, and share thoughts, opinions, and facts impact students who need hope, promise, and purpose. Certainly, learning lies in the hands of the learner. We acknowledge this when we teach with conation in mind.

Heroic Teachers

Heroic teachers know that success comes from grace, wisdom, and determination. In the process, these teachers must rebuild their shattered beliefs, roll up their sleeves, and get to work. Heroic teachers arrive at school each day—sometimes tired but always ready for whatever the day may bring.

Most students are inspired by the strength of their teachers' courage, insight, and will. Students learn quickly that these teachers can't be fooled by the masks students wear. These teachers can see behind the masks of anger, inattention, disruptive behavior, disinterest, and low test scores. They know students use these masks to hide what they don't know and are afraid to ask. They know students don't want to be ridiculed. They understand that masks are an easy way out of learning. They also know the masks hide students' true identity and cover up their conation.

Courageous teachers never stop seeking out and nurturing students' strengths. They seek to understand why certain gaps exist in students' learning and how to build bridges. They recognize teaching is not something they do *to* students; it's a journey they take *with* students. Students need responsible adults who reach out and demonstrate what it means to learn and apply new learning to life. Exemplary teachers strengthen students' assets by focusing on purposeful learning strategies that engage all students through various learning styles. Heroic teachers are heroes because they don't give up on those who have given up on themselves. They step out into the unknown void, probing for the hand, mind, and heart of that student who has been mentally, socially, and emotionally abandoned. They reach out, grab hold, and promise not to let go until this student can find her or his own wings. As evidenced by the following story, students not only discover they can fly above the low expectations and disappointments; not only are they able to fly, but they reach back, grab another student's hand, and together they soar! Read Annette's story.

Back in 1974 when I was in high school, it was a struggle. I had attended one high school that all of my older siblings attended and I was the one asked to leave. It was a parochial school and I barely got in anyway. My scores on the entrance test did not even hit a passing mark, but since my older siblings had been such "great students," I was able to fly in on their sleeves. About halfway through, I was asked to leave by the Dean of Students. I had visited this disciplinarian quite a few times during my freshman year and she finally made a decision for me to move to another school. I was "not" freshman academic material for "their" school. So, little defiant one was sent to Public School!!! A really big disappointment for the Wiederholt Family!! How would they repair the Wiederholt's name after their youngest was asked to be removed from a Parochial School? Oh My Lord!

When I arrived at the local public school, I was naturally placed into all of the lowest academic classes and an adaptive PE class that was devastating. Being the defiant one, I would ditch that class and go to sit in with a friend that I had met and she was taking a Biology course. Miss Fisher was the neatest biology teacher ever. She allowed me to sit in her class, not registered, and she never said no. Everyday that I ditched, she always welcomed me, she greeted me with the same tone of kindness as if I was her student. One day she was headed to the teacher workroom, piled high with work, and she stopped to see just how I was doing. She greeted me, spent time talking to me, and wished me a good day. I was not even a student of hers, but she took the time to talk to me!

This is the impact that I promised myself to be when I became a teacher. Today, I tell all of my students, my door is always open. I have an open door policy and all students are welcome. Many times a day, when a student is bored, they will come to sit in my class to visit and just spend time talking, or on the way to the restroom, they will take the long way, step in, wave hi, and be on their way.

I have created my teaching experience with my students at Mountain View the same way as Miss Fisher did with me. I have been nicknamed Miss Dub, for Miss Wiederholt, since they cannot pronounce Wiederholt. I can be clear across campus and my students will yell excitedly, "Hey Miss Dub." Why? Because I listen to them, I allow them to create conversation with me, and I make no judgment. I allow them to be who they are and I give them my whole attention, just like Miss Fisher did with me!

Miss Annette Wiederholt
High School Math Teacher
Mountain View High School, El Monte, CA

POSITIVE AND NEGATIVE INFLUENCES IMPACT STUDENT LEARNING

We sometimes experience the negative side of human behavior in the actions of students. This misbehavior often results from the actual or perceived lack of positive nurturing and empowerment from significant others. Because the operational framework that governs the overall thinking in our culture is "he who dies with the most toys wins," one of our challenges as educators is to help students expand their thinking about life, education, and future goals. The negative social realities that exist in many of our schools are merely a reflection of the myriad of mixed messages students receive every day.

Three of the most common influences that negatively impact learning and student behavior are anger, apathy, and fear. Often there are variations and combinations of personal issues that block learning (see Figure 5.1).

USING STARS TO SUPPORT THE WILL TO LEARN

Do you ever feel disqualified from being successful? Are you ever overtaken by a sense of uselessness or overwhelmed by feelings of inadequacy? There are times when teachers and students express insecurity.

As a teacher, sometimes you might think that you have students who really don't want to learn or have anything to do with school. Perhaps that is true for some students. So, what can you do? Use the STARS formula shown in Figure 5.3. STARS is an acronym for the factors that support and enhance conative fitness, academic energy, and high performance.

IMPLEMENTING THE FOUR I'S OF TEACHER LEADERSHIP

Effective teachers engage all students in classroom activities by inspiring, informing, investing in, and involving students (see Figure 5.4). First, teachers inspire students to feel that they are part of something special. Students become inspired by their own desire to learn and by the teacher's commitment to the student. Second, teachers inform students through open and honest communication about goals, objectives, assignments, and expected outcomes. However, this communication should be a "two way street" in that students are allowed to communicate to, with, and back to the teacher, what they understand or do not understand, which strategies and activities are more interesting and engaging, and what "turns them on to learning." Effective teachers are willing to receive communication from students as well as convey it. Third, teachers invest in students by letting them know we want them to succeed in school and

Figure 5.1   Intrinsic Negative Influences That Impact Student Learning

Anger/Frustration

Feeling	*Thinking*	*Acting*
Resentful	Don't tell me what to do!	Rude
Annoyed	Why do we have to do this stuff?	Stubborn
Irritated	Nobody ever listens to me.	Passive-Aggressive
Disgusted	That's it! I'm not doing anything else!	Defiant!
Furious	You better get away from me!	Destructive
_____	_____	_____
_____	_____	_____
_____	_____	_____

Apathy/Boredom

Feeling	*Thinking*	*Acting*
Numb	It really doesn't matter	Listless
Helpless	I don't know how.	Stuck
Powerless	No way, forget it.	Spaced out
Tired	I don't know why I even come to school.	Indifferent
Depressed	It's no use.	Unresponsive
_____	_____	_____
_____	_____	_____
_____	_____	_____

Fear/Insecurity

Feeling	*Thinking*	*Acting*
Anxious	What if I don't get it right?	Hyperactive
Confused	I don't know what to do.	Overwhelmed
Uncertain	What if I fail?	Nervous
Threatened	I wish I were someplace else.	Scared
Dread	My life depends on this test and I'm not ready.	Traumatized
_____	_____	_____
_____	_____	_____
_____	_____	_____

Figure 5.2   Intrinsic Positive Influences That Impact Student Learning

Competence/Confidence

Feeling	Thinking	Acting
Capable	I understand the assignment.	Learning, seeks to live up to potential, asks questions
Acceptance of self	I will give my best.	Putting forth consistent effort, overcoming peer pressure
Inner peace	I can learn this and I will.	Engaged, gives personal best
Personal control	I need to make a plan.	Working toward and achieving learning goals
Curious	I will ask questions.	Listening/paying attention, getting the job done
_____	_____	_____
_____	_____	_____
_____	_____	_____
_____	_____	_____
_____	_____	_____

Courage/Commitment

Feeling	Thinking	Acting
Enthusiastic	I'm looking forward to learning.	Works hard, gives 100%
Inspired	I know what I want to do with this project.	Involved, stays on task, values learning
Creative	I want my work to stand out and be excellent.	Excited, engaged, discovers personal strengths
Optimistic	I'm going to take some risks.	Volunteers/participates, goes against the odds
Determined to learn	I will learn in spite of any challenges.	Tries new learning experiences, makes rewarding decisions, stays on task
_____	_____	_____
_____	_____	_____
_____	_____	_____
_____	_____	_____
_____	_____	_____

(Continued)

Figure 5.2   (Continued)

Character/Caring		
Feeling	*Thinking*	*Acting*
Hopeful	I have never done this before but I know I will do well in this class.	Talks to the teacher about progress, makes changes as necessary
Resilient	Things don't always go well for me in school but I'm not giving up.	Bounces back, winning attitude, seeks personal growth
Supportive	I will work together with others. I will be a resource.	Helpful to self and others, chooses to be successful, empathetic
Responsible	I'm going to learn this for me.	Dependable, turns assignments in on time
Respectful	I know what I must do and I will learn all that I can.	Accepts standards and expectations, works toward assigned and personal goals, values learning

Figure 5.3   The STARS of Conative Fitness

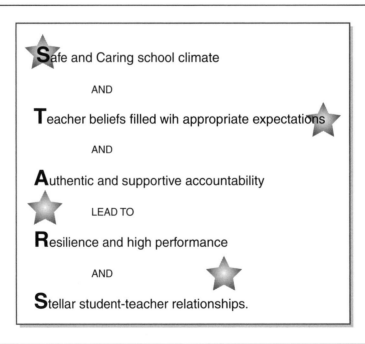

Safe and Caring school climate

AND

Teacher beliefs filled wih appropriate expectations

AND

Authentic and supportive accountability

LEAD TO

Resilience and high performance

AND

Stellar student-teacher relationships.

Figure 5.4 The Four I's of Teacher Leadership

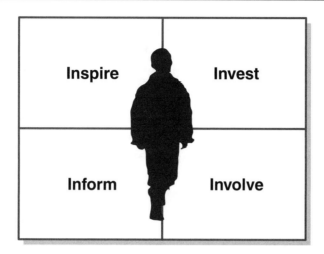

life, and that we are available to support their efforts and facilitate their learning. We demonstrate the belief that our investment in them has merit and will yield a significant return by listening to their concerns, problems, and input and by recognizing their accomplishments, accepting their failures, and appreciating their individual personalities and abilities. Fourth, teachers involve students by bringing them together to share projects, activities, and ideas. Students build peer relationships through academic and social interactions. Teachers also involve students by strengthening student-teacher relationships.

The Will to Succeed

A New Day in Education

The magic of successful learning organizations can be experienced by watching the spontaneity of excitement in students' eyes and by listening to their conversations. When we take time to reflect on what is being taught and learned, we transform the old into new and the new into dreams that can be realized tomorrow. Mindful teaching moves learning beyond the simplicity of busywork into realms of new possibilities.

PROMOTING CONATION SCHOOL-WIDE

It is not enough to promote conation in the classroom, we must also promote it throughout the school. Many schools are engaged in systemic change initiatives. Conation should be part of these initiatives.

Who Needs Assessments?

To promote conation school-wide, we must examine how well we are meeting students' needs through our systemic change initiatives. How many needs assessments have you read (or written) regarding desired changes and outcomes for your school or organization? In many schools across the nation, there is a need for systemic change. As we seek change, we must also reflect and respond to this question: How much growth has taken place in my school in the past few years? It is critical that we take time to examine the accomplishments and recognize the practices and people who promoted the change process.

The Will to Succeed

The Spirit of Conation

We can know who we are and we can realize our own power if we take time to find ourselves and acknowledge our power in the present moment. Our power is available right here, where we live and breathe, hope and dream. In the present moment, we can challenge and demand ourselves and others to be the best we can be. This is the spirit of conation.

We can examine our schools through growth assessments. A growth assessment allows us to do the following:

- Examine where we are
- Determine collectively if where we are is where we should be at this point in time
- Value our achievements (no matter how great or small)
- Ascertain whether or not our accomplishments align with our goals
- Reassess where we are going
- Evaluate how far we have come
- Build upon our strengths
- Celebrate our accomplishments
- Seek and use new team-building strategies
- Explore new possibilities
- Make adjustments for continuous growth

We must regularly determine what students need to know in order to succeed in our global economy. Our school agendas must reflect the conative idea that transformational learning happens when teachers have the *will* and *determination* to teach every student with no exceptions.

Building Conation Into the Curriculum

Another way to promote conation school-wide is to include conation in the curriculum. By building a conative connection into the curriculum, teachers alter the self-repression dynamic and, instead, construct paradigms for maximal student development. When students are taught in a harmonious, mutually respectful environment, they change their behavior and increase their participation in learning. Many students want to perform well, but are often discouraged by hostile and stressful conditions at home, with peers, in school, or within themselves. The way teachers invite (or "disinvite") students to participate in classroom learning speaks volumes about what and whom they value, who they believe will or will not learn, and who deserves their support. School achievement and self-respect (viewing oneself as intellectually, emotionally, and socially capable) are not separate issues, but shared goals.

The Will to Succeed

Looking Back

Examine your life. Remember you have reached the place you are right now—whether good or not so good—through the actions you've taken based on your beliefs, values, life experiences, perceptions of yourself, perceptions of the world around you, and strength of will.

Reaching Past Fear and Doubt

In learning and in life, adults create the experiences, climate, and conditions in which students live and learn. If we find it difficult to imagine our own goals and dreams, then we must take time to chart new beginnings and write new chapters for ourselves. We must infuse ourselves with courage—courage to see positive outcomes in our lives and courage to realize and live out our deepest beliefs and values. Courage enables us to transcend our fears and doubts and to strive toward our personal beliefs, values, and goals.

When we wonder why some students fail and others succeed, we must remember the role that students' belief systems play in achievement. We must also examine our willingness to nurture positive beliefs if we wish to promote maximal performance. When students respect themselves and we nurture that self-respect, students will be successful in their academic performance. Conation is the foundation that determines if students will choose to strive, give up, or work somewhere in between.

For generations we have developed and reformed learning systems, but we've forgotten to use one of our greatest tools for effecting change—conation. We use conation in the classroom and curriculum, but forget to use it in our systemic change initiatives and in our everyday lives. If we want to be truly lifelong learners, why not strive to be the best we can be? Why not open our hearts and minds to fresh ideas, new possibilities, and the *will* to discover authentic success beyond the limitations we place on ourselves and our students?

Figure 5.5 Grow the Power

Schools can grow the power of personal achievement by

- modeling,
- supporting,
- guiding,
- caring,
- expecting,
- acknowledging, and
- preparing students to succeed in the best and worst conditions at school, at home, and in everyday life.

Schools can grow students' power to succeed by promoting conation. Ideas for growing this power are shown in Figure 5.5.

KEEP REACHING AND THEN JUST . . . KEEP ON TEACHING!

Both teachers and students are driven by the *will*. A hero resides in every teacher and student. Classrooms are filled with everyday heroes. Sometimes the heroes fall asleep, because we forget to invite them into our lives (see Figure 5.6). Will we allow the hero to craft new thinking and actions in our expectations and work with students?

Think of each day as a new beginning in some child's life. You *do* make a difference. You have the power to help unleash the hero from deep within your students. The hero (power within) is often held hostage by negative beliefs. Help them uncover their inner hero. Once in touch with the power within, they can choose to succeed.

Figure 5.6 Just Keep on Teaching

When students come from communities
that are exploding with anger, outrage, or fear,
 just keep on teaching.

When students come from homes where love has been abandoned
and dismantled by apathy, hopelessness, and despair,
 just keep on teaching.

When hate is just another four-letter word,
where lives are put on hold and dreams are deferred,
just keep on teaching.

When students explain
that the meaning of hope is as foreign as the meaning of truth,
 just keep on teaching.

When students' lives are fragmented,
when they don't know to whom they can turn,
when they're lost in the shadows of those who know longer dream of what can be,
step back, regroup, start teaching, and
 just keep on teaching.

When you work with parents whose minds are washed by television soaps,
dulled by a residue of emptiness and an inability to cope,
when ambitions are discarded by promises gone astray—
they want better for their children, but they don't know of any other way—
teach them how promises are fulfilled,
through hard work, determination, and a never-ending will.
 Just keep on teaching.

Growing up too fast, adult experiences too soon,
lives so young—but not so tender.
Where are the children?
You pause and remember that you must
 just keep on teaching.

(Continued)

Figure 5.6   (Continued)

Alcohol-stained lives, drugs, gangs, and guns on the rise,
tension in the air and war in the streets, cries for help.
You reach some, and others you must let go,
the pain of their lifestyles weigh heavy on your soul.
Exhausted, but there you are,
a mystery of goodness, nobility of action, still giving—
    just keep on teaching.

Children wanting to belong,
thinking macho and "using" means being strong.
    Just keep on teaching.

Incomprehensible is what you describe
as you look at so many of your students' lives.
If you don't reach them, who will?
    Just keep on teaching.

Becoming involved in guiding their way
Sometimes gets hard as you help them make it through each day.
    Just keep on teaching.

Inspiring students to reach up high,
because that's the place where their futures lie—
if they are to succeed, you can't give up.
    Just keep on teaching.

Experiencing the feeling of doing something right,
perhaps for the first time in all of their lives,
Profound and personal, you are encouraging kids
to believe in themselves and then achieve.
    Just keep on teaching.

You are the human voice, cultivating the winner within—
the hero some call it.
You've done it before, and you can do it again,
    just keep on teaching.

E ducation is not limited to a stu-

dent learning how to read, write, or
think critically, but it includes teaching students about interpersonal and intrapersonal relationships. Education should prepare
students emotionally, psychologically, and intellectually. It is vital
that students acquire core knowledge and skills, but it is also an
essential part of their education to learn how to get along with
and relate to others in a socially coexistent relationship.

The following lessons are designed to help students understand relationships and their importance. The lessons motivate
students to read stories and novels focusing on a historic context, but also encourage them to examine their feelings and
beliefs about themselves and their interactions with others.

THINK ABOUT IT!

The most important ingredient in the formula of success is knowing how to get along with people.

—Theodore Roosevelt

WHAT'S IT ALL ABOUT?

Grade Level: Primary

Purpose

- To help students become aware of their relationships with friends, family members, teachers, and others
- To develop students' awareness of and belief in their ability to solve problems
- To help students discover their own abilities to cope with challenges
- To make students aware of their abilities to succeed in life and school

Instructional Objectives

- Students will develop an understanding of the importance of relationships with others.
- Students will develop critical thinking skills through interactions with real-life situations and through literature.
- Students will enhance their knowledge and understanding of themselves.
- Students will gain an understanding of their beliefs about themselves and their gifts, skills, talents, and abilities.

Interdisciplinary Implementation

- Conflict resolution
- Career education
- Language arts
- Technology
- Reading

Instructional Focus

Students will complete the Semantic Feature Analysis and will improve their abilities in:

- Making inferences,
- Applying metacognition,
- Accessing prior knowledge, and
- Using critical thinking.

MAKING THE CONNECTION

Instructional Strategies and Activities

1. As a class, read "The Little Red Hen" or a similar story that features the theme of relationships between people or animals.
2. Encourage students to compare the Little Red Hen's attitude and behavior to the attitudes and behaviors of the other animals.
   a. Draw a Semantic Feature Analysis chart (as shown on the next page) to help students determine specific traits about the various animals.
   b. Discuss each animal's attitudes and behaviors. Ask students to designate the traits each animal exhibited by placing a mark in the appropriate boxes on the chart.
3. Ask students: Why do you think the duck (cat, dog) was unhelpful (uncooperative, inconsiderate, etc.)?
4. Challenge students to examine their own attitudes and behaviors:
   a. Are there times when you are unhelpful (uncaring, uncooperative, etc.)?
   b. What can you do to correct your actions?
5. Encourage students to name the good character traits that the Little Red Hen possessed.

Semantic Feature Analysis

Animals	Helpful	Unhelpful	Cooperative	Uncooperative	Caring	Uncaring	Considerate
Duck							
Cat							
Dog							
Little Red Hen							

CONATIVE INSIGHT: Now that I *know*, what will I do?

Extended Research and Reflection

Challenge students to retell this story by drawing their own pictures of what happened. Explain that the pictures should be placed in sequence according to the events that took place in the story.

Encourage students to reflect on their learning by answering the following questions:

1. What did you learn from the story?
2. Why do you think that the Little Red Hen did not become discouraged when none of the other animals would help?
3. Was it fair of the Little Red Hen to refuse to share the bread with the other animals? Explain your answer.

ASSESSMENT

Assess the success of the lesson by asking yourself the following questions:

1. Did students participate in the oral discussions?
2. Were students able to retell the story correctly in their drawings?
3. Did students exhibit an understanding of the significance of the story?
4. Were students able to relate and reflect on their own behaviors and traits?

WHAT IF . . . ?

History, despite its wrenching pain, cannot be unlived, but if faced with courage, need not be lived again.

—Maya Angelou

WHAT'S IT ALL ABOUT

Grade Level: Elementary, Middle, and High School

Purpose

- To promote students' interest in historical events and people
- To help students, through authentic tasks, understand how the past can affect the present
- To encourage students to use their creative and critical thinking skills

Instructional Objectives

- Students will develop a knowledge base about historical events and people.
- Students will become more interested in history.
- Students will connect historical events to current events.

Interdisciplinary Implementation

- History
- Language arts
- Career development
- Character education

Instructional Focus

Students will read the special report on the Civil War and reflect on the following issues:

- how the outcomes of historical events have impacted on current events,
- how history can teach us how to prepare for a better future, and
- why learning and knowing about history can be interesting and informative.

MAKING THE CONNECTION

Instructional Strategies and Activities

1. Explain to students that an important project has been assigned to station INFORM-TV. The station is accepting applications for these positions:

   - Reporter
   - News writer
   - Editor
   - Television producer
   - Researcher
   - Graphic artist
   - Television news anchor

   List the positions on the board and ask each student to select the job(s) for which they wish to apply. Explain that more than one person can work at each job.

2. Challenge students to apply for the jobs by writing a letter to the executive producer that explains why they would like a certain position, their qualifications, and why they would be the best person for the position. Ask the class to determine how applicants will be selected.

3. Explain that this project involves "reconstructing" history. Tell students to choose a particular event in history from the Historical Events list (on the next page) You can also encourage students to think of other events they might like to study.

4. If students do not know the details about this event, encourage them to do some research. (Remember, a primary purpose of this lesson is to challenge students to broaden their knowledge base about historical events.) Discuss what led up to the event, what incidents occurred, and the outcome.

5. Challenge students to explain what they think the country, the world, or the fate of certain racial or religious groups might be today if things had turned out differently. (For an example, see the Special Report on page 133.)

6. Place students in teams. Try to have as many of the roles (editor, graphic artist, etc.) represented in each group as possible.

7. Challenge teams to gather information about the event and then rewrite and reconstruct the event. In other words, students will take a quantum leap or travel on a time machine

back to the event and change the face of history. Encourage teams to make graphics to illustrate their stories.

8. When teams are finished, ask the news anchors to present the team reports.

Historical Events

American colonies win independence from England

North defeats the South in the Civil War

Japan bombs Pearl Harbor

Great Depression of 1929

Mass production of the automobile

Mexican revolution

Dropping of the atomic bomb at Hiroshima

Industrial Revolution

Bay of Pigs

Harlem Renaissance

Internment of Japanese-Americans

The Holocaust

Special Report

The South has won the Civil War! Confederate soldiers were victorious over the ill-prepared Union Army. The surviving Northern troops are preparing to gather their wounded and dead and return to their homes in the North. As a result of this astounding victory, there will be no changes in the current policy regarding the owning of slaves.

Now the South can return to its regal way of life. We can start to rebuild our plantations, get our crops planted, and continue the way of life that our ancestors left us as a rightful legacy and that we can now leave to our children and our children's children.

We will continue to take care of our slaves as we have always done. We will ensure that they are fed, clothed, and cared for as long as they remain our property and on our plantations. They are happy with their way of life and did not welcome the changes that President Lincoln tried to force on them. We are happy that the South will be able to resume our beautiful way of life. Long live the South!

CONATIVE INSIGHT: Now that I *know*, what will I do?

Extended Research and Reflection

1. Ask students to reread this quote by Maya Angelou: "History, despite its wrenching pain, cannot be unlived, but if faced with courage, need not be lived again." Challenge students to research Maya Angelou's life and answer the following questions:

   a. What is her profession, career, or vocation?

   b. What are her beliefs, values, and views about life, the world, and people?

   c. What are some other books, poems, and statements made by Maya Angelou that provide insight into her character, convictions, and viewpoints?

   d. How does her writing reflect her beliefs and values?

2. Use the graphic organizer on the next page to depict the causes and effects of a historical event that the class is currently studying or has studied in the past.

Ask students to think about some positive deed they did that resulted in making someone happy, or caused some changes either in their lives or someone else's life.

Ask students to think about a famous person in history they may have read about and reflect on the following questions:

1. What character traits did this person possess?

2. Do you think his or her traits contributed to this person's accomplishments or actions? Explain how.

3. Did this person have traits that you would like to have, or that you possibly already possess? Explain your answer.

4. Do you think your famous person in history could have achieved what he or she did without the character traits you named? Explain your answer.

Cause and Effect Graphic Organizer

Cause
The events that happened were:

Effect
As a result, this is what happened:

Write a summary, listing the primary causes or events that took place, leading to or resulting in the _____.

List and explain the effects these events had on _____'s history then and now.

ASSESSMENT

Assess the success of the lesson by asking yourself the following questions:

1. How did students use their writing skills?
2. How did students demonstrate their decision-making skills?
3. How well were teams able to work together?
4. Did students increase their knowledge about historical events, people, and places? How was this knowledge demonstrated?

Something Dropped a Song in My Heart

Teaching Conation Through Music and Creative Writing

The role of music and writing in structuring teaching in the conative domain, especially the creation of lyrics, is an excellent instructional vehicle for making students aware of their strengths and growth potential. Conative development through music, along with the integration of positive values about self throughout all content areas such as reading, math, science, social studies, liberal arts, history, literature, and humanities can set the climate for overall school success.

Through the creation and writing of lyrics, students can express their dreams, their future, and their own reality. Sound instruction in music education opens doors for engaging students in higher order thinking skills with applications that relate to social, emotional, and academic well-being. In writing lyrics, students are challenged to create words of hope, determination, love and respect for self and others, and courage to overcome adversities in school and life. The common theme that runs through our body of literature involving conation and its impact on schools is that learning is a personal enterprise. Certainly music is a transmitter of values and virtues, culture and character.

Curriculum that builds upon how students see themselves and the world around them through song and imagination can reshape their thinking about who they are and their significance to society. If our goal as educators is to inspire students to become positive and self-directed about life and learning, music is certainly a tremendous beginning, a way of getting the process started. Music can foster a proactive approach for establishing a framework in which productive intentional behavior can thrive, igniting the fires of change from within. Music designed for a positive purpose, like seeds, help students grow in ways that may seem amazing to those who take time to cultivate resilience and direction.

Music has a way of bringing to the forefront the vitality that resides within; the zest, the gusto, the creativity, drive, and determination. Life-building music reminds us to seek light and then build around it. As a metaphor, light bridges darkness, moving one beyond the limiting confines of negative behavior, if one chooses to release the light from within. Songs, when played again and again at the will of the learner (even in the learner's thoughts), offer strength and peace in a world that is often challenging, and sometimes uninviting. An ability to interpret—to stop, to think, to ponder, to wrestle with the creation of lyrics for a song, as much as sing it—is fundamentally useful to the learner in a self-instructional manner as to how "things" can change.

The language of music can encourage the heart of the learner to think, act, and achieve higher levels of knowing and being. Through teaching learning as intentional behavior that needs to be nurtured, students can be encouraged to develop attitudes and dispositions for learning that hopefully will cause them to value themselves, education, and the world in which they live. As active participants, observers, and listeners, students can visualize themselves through lyrics, making a difference in a world that offers so many opportunities. Students can write their own stories with personal thoughts that highlight their dreams and aspirations. Conative music is engaging, effective, and can be curriculum-based. Students can be taught to write songs, compose music, choreograph dances, teach sign language, and more that will help them analyze the meaning of their lives, education, and the future.

There are numerous ways to teach conation through music when it is integrated throughout the curriculum. Through creating songs, dances, and time for reflection, bringing students face-to-face with choices and challenges, real and imagined, they can alter their educational journeys, making their lives richer, deeper, thoughtful, and profound. When the unstoppable rise from within to succeed breaks the barriers of limited goals or no goals at all, students realize from this point on there is "no turning back."

Music can help students touch their lives in very tangible ways; it can help students unfold, and evolve into more of who they truly are. Music holds the power to move us and then make us move in better and more humane ways. Truth, goodness, liberation, and self-determination are recurring themes in conative building music; a gift that helps some youth untangle their lives. The journey begins at the marrow of learning, taking students to bold new worlds and places that many would never know without the powerful simplicity of a "life-giving" song.

SOMETHING DROPPED A SONG IN MY HEART

A song has a few rights the same as ordinary citizens . . . if it happens to feel like flying where humans cannot fly . . . to scale mountains that are not there, who shall stop it?

—Charles Ives

WHAT'S IT ALL ABOUT?

Grade Level: Elementary, Middle, and High School

Purpose

- To promote students' appreciation for the arts
- To introduce students to the relevance of other subjects in addition to core content subjects
- To encourage students to tap into their multiple intelligences
- To encourage students to use their higher order thinking skills

Instructional Objectives

- Students will be able to listen to different genres of songs, and identify and analyze the various moods represented.
- Students will understand the term "lyrics" and be able to apply it to a writing assignment.
- Students will develop an appreciation for songs from other cultures.
- Students will be able to express feelings or emotions through the skill of writing.
- Students will learn the skill of creating lyrics from their authentic writings.
- Students will learn the skill and joy of song writing as another means of effective communication.
- Students will learn how to use music as a vehicle to express their joys, frustrations, failures, successes, and determination to overcome adversities.

Interdisciplinary Implementation

- History
- English
- Character education
- Cultural awareness
- Technology

Instructional Focus

Using music through song writing is an authentic performance task, as well as an inspiring vehicle to capturing the interest of students and motivating them to "want to write." Music is their life! It is what they do! Just look around. If you are in a mall, near a school, or any place where young people congregate, you will observe nine out of ten of them walking around with some form of musical apparatus connected to their ears. There is something in the songs that draws one to this particular venue; that causes a connection, bonding, emotional interaction, and a nonthreatening conduit for expressing oneself. As stated on one Web site:

When creating music we have the ability to convey a feeling, mood, or emotion. As a result, music can have many different effects on individuals, groups, and society as a whole. Some believe that listening to music can reduce stress, help increase your recovery time when having an operation, and even raise test scores!

—www.powertolearn.com/themes_music/genres.html

As previously stated, students love music, but too often their knowledge is limited to one or two genres. One of the goals of education is to help students become knowledgeable about the world around them; to expand their horizons, hopes, and dreams beyond the confines of their environment, and to enhance their awareness of the richness of all kinds of music.

MAKING THE CONNECTION

Instructional Strategies and Activities

1. Have students form cooperative teams.
2. Have students create two semantic webs. Title one as **Types of songs or music I like**; the other as **Types of music I know about.**
3. Have the teams brainstorm, using the webs to record their responses.
4. Have the teams compare their webs. Check to see if they have included various genres of songs listed below or others that may represent their culture or ethnicity. Some examples are:
   - Folk
   - Country & Western
   - Jazz
   - Reggae
   - Blues
   - Hip hop
   - Rock
   - Classical
   - Religious
   - Asian
   - Caribbean
   - Polish
   - Rap
   - Pop
5. Have a sampling of different songs on DVDs whose words represent a variety of moods or emotions, have positive or negative messages, or have the effect of eliciting certain reactions from students.
6. Have students discuss, analyze, and formulate inferences regarding the type of message each song is conveying.
7. Ask students guiding questions such as:
   - What kind of message did you get out of this song?
   - How do you think the artist was feeling when he or she wrote this song? Give a rationale for your answer.
   - How did this song make you feel? Why?

- Do you think the words of songs have the power to make you feel a certain way? How? Give a rationale for your answer.
- Do you think writing your feelings as words of a song will help you communicate to others how you feel, what you think about things, and what dreams and desires you want for your future? Why? How?

8. Have students, in their teams:

   ♪ Select a topic,

   ♪ Compose (write a song focusing on the topic),

   ♪ Make up a melody or beat for their song, and

   ♪ Perform their song for the other teams.

9. Discuss the rationale, process, and what was learned from this activity.

CONATIVE INSIGHT: Now that I *know*, what will I do?

Extended Research and Reflection

1. Have students use the Internet or library to research information about the importance and impact music has on our daily lives.

2. Have students select one genre of music and conduct research on its origin.

ASSESSMENT

Each student will compose a song that focuses on his or her aspirations for the future. Share with them that the words of their song should be positive, should express hope, and should exhibit their willingness to work hard in order to achieve their goals in life.

WHAT'S IN A WORD?

Did is a word of achievement; **won't** is a word of retreat; **might** is a word of bereavement; **can't** is a word of defeat; **ought** is a word of duty; **try** is a word each hour; **will** is a word of beauty; **can** is a word of power!

—Author Unknown

WHAT'S IT ALL ABOUT?

Grade Level: Elementary, Middle, and High School

Purpose

- To acquaint students with the power of words and language
- To enhance students' self-efficacy
- To provide students with a better understanding of the concept of conation through the utilization of a lexicon

Instructional Objectives

- Students will promote critical thinking skills.
- Students will enhance writing skills.
- Students will engage in expository reading.

Interdisciplinary Implementation

- Vocabulary
- Literacy skills
- Technology
- Science
- Math
- History

Instructional Focus

Students will conduct research on or read an autobiography or biography about one nonfictional person who at some time in his/her life:

- Was confronted with one or more challenging episodes or events,
- Felt no one loved or cared about them,
- Thought no one was willing to help them,

- Was told they would never succeed or "amount to anything," or
- Believed no one had faith or confidence in their ability to overcome or succeed in spite of their problems.

MAKING THE CONNECTION

Instructional Strategies and Activities

Part I

Students will:

- Refer to the lexicon on pages 147–148 and read the various terms and phrases listed;
- Select and list between 15–25 of these terms, attributes, character traits, and/or phrases that describe the qualities, will, and determination possessed by this individual that enabled him/her to overcome or "beat the odds";
- Use their selection of words to write and explain how each term helped this person to succeed in his/her endeavor; and
- Share their projects orally with classmates.

Part II

Students will:

- Think of one personal obstacle or challenge they have experienced;
- Select terms, attributes, and/or phrases from the lexicon that will help describe their strengths and the character traits they possessed that helped them overcome or succeed in spite of these problems;
- Write and explain how each of these terms helped him/her realize they had the will, persistence, and power to successfully "deal with the problem"; and
- Share their personal stories.

CONATIVE INSIGHT: Now that I *know*, what will I do?

Extended Research and Reflection

Have students form cooperative teams. Each team will select a historical individual or someone current, who had in the past or in recent times, experienced problems in their lives but were able to overcome them. Teams will share, and then have a class discussion focusing on the inner strengths each person possessed and how these strengths helped them to survive and succeed.

Have students discuss how these examples can be applied to their lives. Ask if they have some of the common traits these people had/have. Ask them to reflect on their own abilities they use on a daily basis to help themselves address and solve life's problems, be they large or small.

Lesson Extension

The lexicon used in this lesson is quite extensive, with more than two hundred words, thoughts, phrases, attitudes and expectations that contribute to helping students better understand the concept of conation and how it directly relates to their lives through these conative connections.

There are also numerous and creative ways this lexicon can be used which will address and support your state's standards and required direct teaching of specified skills, i.e., writing, reading, and higher order thinking. A few suggestions are:

- Assign a word or phrase each day or week from the lexicon. Have students write an expository, narrative, descriptive, or persuasive paragraph; or a story, poem, prose, song, and rap; or even create an artistic representation of their thoughts . . . whatever venue they select. This will give each student an opportunity to tap into his/her particular multiple intelligence(s). This activity will also give second-language students an opportunity to acquire, use, and expand on their existing skills and knowledge.

- Have students create a daily or weekly journal in which they write their thoughts and feelings about the selected word or phrase and how this relates to their life, plans for the future, and expectations.

- Integrate terms with content area subjects such as history, social studies, science, mathematics, and English by having students make connections with people they read about in these subjects.
- Have them identify, explain, compare, and examine the qualities, gifts, talents, skills, and other attributes of these people that enabled them to make sacrifices, save their countries, contribute to society in some significant manner, or just made themselves a better person through their own will and determination.

ASSESSMENT

Informally assess this lesson by asking students the following questions:

- What new definitions, words, and phrases did you learn as you utilized the lexicon?
- Can you explain, in your words, what conation means? Do you feel differently about yourself? How? Why? In what way(s)?
- Do you now have a better idea of how words can convey powerful images about a person? Explain your answer with some specific examples from our class discussions.

A LEXICON OF TWO HUNDRED WORDS, THOUGHTS, PHRASES, ATTITUDES, AND EXPECTATIONS THAT BUILD CONATIVE CONNECTIONS

Hopeful learners—engaged teachers—courageous students—remarkable role models—heroic classrooms—great listeners—giving their best—enlightening others—building—stretching—growing—listening—hearing—caring—connecting—supporting—sharing—strengthening—helping—releasing—striving—working—setting goals—building lives—believing—hoping—moving forward—thoughtful persuasion—compassion—determination—holding on—letting go—reaching—finding answers—focusing on what's important—choosing priorities—being fully present in the moment—lifting others as you climb—setting worthy goals—cheering students on—making learning fun—finding joy—doing something you've never tried before—engaging—enhancing—restoring—renewing—making the best of a bad situation—falling down, getting up—starting all over again—thinking—exploring—demonstrating—celebrating—including—anticipating—making a difference—finding common ground—bringing out the best—taking ownership—challenging oneself—modifying instruction—changing beliefs—changing actions—shifting paradigms—enlightening—welcoming—encouraging—embracing—doing what's right—being grateful—a positive sense of self and others—mutual respect—empathy—responsible behavior—responsive teaching—choosing the greatest good—lifelong learning—stamina—going against the odds—courage—consistency—patience—quality instruction—giving students a voice—trust—ownership—effort—intentional learning—honesty—openness—sense of belonging—the WOW effect—Experience the moment—You are special—Great work—incredible—I'm proud of you—I feel your joy—I know your pain—This is the me I've always wanted to be—I knew I could do it—You deserve the best—I feel so free—friends—hope—smiles—yes!—remarkable—excellent—Your ideas are important—Tell me more—super!—wonderful!—I can't wait to see your next project—We're a team—Plan to succeed!—You're a winner—Keep up the good work—fantastic—You're the best—I respect you—You give me joy—What a class!—Extraordinary teachers see the future in the eyes of their students—I wouldn't trade my students for anything in the world—You gave it a good try—When you fail, get up and try again—I love your honesty—

Let's work on this together—You can do it— You're getting there—You did it!— Terrific—Thanks!—I can always count on you—It wasn't easy, but you hung in there—You own the power!—I appreciate you—Keep standing up for what you believe in—Hold on to your dreams—Never stop growing—Never stop wanting to give more—wanting to know more—wanting to be more—If you need me, I am available—We're in this together—You have purpose—You have meaning—You are significant—We all get frustrated sometimes—When you release doubt, anger, and fear, you're no longer the same—new directions—impulse control—Life takes on new meaning—It's great to be alive—Laugh a lot—It protects you from hardening of the heart—Laugh until you cry—Be silly—Witness the impossible with awe, wonder, and praise—Lead the possible—Remember obedience to the unenforceable—Obey the good that lives in you—Celebrate small things—Mindfully listen to students—You'll both be amazed—Think big—If you think you can, you can—Never give up on a student!—Never give up on yourself—plan—organize—collaborate—Work it out—Try something new—Make your goals a huge part of your life—Shorten the distance between now and the future—Make outstanding choices everyday—Take charge—If you won't, who will—Build a legacy—Make it great—Challenge yourself—Reinvent your thinking and your actions will follow—It's your turn—It's your time—It's your opportunity—It's your life—Go for it!—Polish your personality with a smile—push—pull—Break barriers—Capture the wisdom of great minds—Be strong—Launch the power—Find yourself turned on by things you never knew, you never knew—Make an exciting contribution—Your purpose and place in life are worth fighting for—Keep the good fights going!—Someone is walking in your light—Keep it shining—Learn—Grow—Become.

6

The Bridge Between the Desire to Achieve and Reality is . . . The Will

Putting It All Together

If I am the Future

If I am the future and upon your shoulders I must stand, guide me with the inner elegance of your wisdom. Patiently share your world with me, gently impressing upon my heart and mind the value of a fulfilled life. Understanding who I am and who you are, I will look up to you—then I will climb.

Share your past with me so that I can understand the present. It is here in the present that we share a common bond. Different ideas perhaps about who we are, but a bond no less that makes us one. The future will become the past, but as time allows, it is yours, it is mine, it is ours to shape and define. I have unlimited energy, you have discernment. Together we will build tomorrow.

Inspire me by your courage to do good then I will know how to speak and walk with integrity. As you seek to know truth, I will gain insight into what is important, and what is not on the journey. Lift me—and I will climb.

Touched by your actions, I will visibly stand high above conflict and confusion. Teach me with words of life uplifting, and I will rise far beyond your expectations, beyond the horizon, I will rise to the place where dreams are born.

Tomorrow's world will be an expression of what we will build together:

Your experience	*My sense of wonder*
Your knowledge	*My willingness to learn*
Your strength	*My flexibility*
Your calm reserve manner	*My love for adventure*
Your clarity	*My voice*
Your technology	*My determination to advance it*
Your being grounded	*My groundbreaking nature*
Your accomplishments	*My desire to achieve*
Your knowledge	*My quest to celebrate*
of the human spirit	*it everyday*
Your being true to what	*My wanting to know what to*
you believe	*believe in*
Your answers	*My questions*
YOUR ROOTS	*MY WINGS*

The journey to the future begins one step at a time. However, time will not wait. We must begin. Are you ready? The future is now!

THE WILL

The will is the place where we discover the strength of what we really want to achieve. If your internal desire to achieve a goal is strong enough for you to take serious action . . . then the will quickly becomes your agent of change working with you from within, enabling you to move forward or to even become unstoppable in your endeavor to achieve your goal.

The resiliency of will acts on your behalf. When you desire to do something, the will is the place where intentional action occurs. However, in order to utilize it, you must first realize that the will resides in the conative domain, a place that exists within you and can be accessed whenever your goal attainment desire is transformed into action.

When the desire to change becomes greater than the desire to stay the same, action takes place and the will goes into full effect, holding us up, keeping us focused and moving forward toward our intended goal. For the most part, we are the only ones who can halt the progress of goal-oriented behavior. If we make a decision to stop working toward a specific goal, the work of the will accordingly stops. It no longer moves us forward in that we have chosen to detach ourselves from the goal. Otherwise the will, when set in motion, continues to work within us if the desire is there, keeping us focused through completion.

THE BRIDGE METAPHOR

The *bridge* reference to the will is significant to the work of the will in that conation or the will enables us to stand tall with endurance and determination to **reach** above, go around or even through what appears to some as obstacles and distractions to teaching and learning. However, sustained momentum to strive is maintained only when we are determined not to quit, but to keep going despite circumstances that appear to get in our way.

Conation itself is what keeps us from quitting. It is always there within us, but too often it goes unnoticed, therefore unutilized, waiting sometimes for a lifetime, to be called to action as an enabler to achieve our desires and goals.

As a bridge, conation has the capacity to take us beyond what may reside around us to places where perhaps we would not venture to experience, would never have known about or how to reach. Without an overpass, a link to new possibilities and an effective means of transportation *(referring to the will)*, achieving a specific goal might be impossible. Conation, as a bridge, is the stamina that supports a desired action over time. It is also the action itself and the driving force that enables us to attempt to make a difference and then carry it through.

Conation tells us a great deal about who we are, what we believe about what is important, what is not, and why. It encourages us to examine how much we are willing to do to accomplish a given goal.

The power of conation is its ability to keep us moving forward, to build and renew a spirit of creativity, capture and initiate a desire for learning, elicit depth and dimension in hard work, connect to relentless strength that rises from within even when our lives are turned upside down. The conative domain when examined is the witness to "why" what happens in the classroom happens on an individual and **collective basis.**

When issues in education focus on a student's ability, i.e., *"to achieve or not to achieve"* and the capacity to learn is not an issue, the real questions become: Has conation been factored into the formula regarding *this* student's success? Does the student have the will to learn? If not, why? What steps should be taken to start the process?

INSIGHTS REGARDING CONATION: NEXT STEPS

Throughout this book, as a facilitator of learning, you have been asked to look at teaching and learning through a different lens that you may not be familiar or even comfortable with; however, you have been encouraged to reflect on "doing school differently" that will, hopefully, result in a more supportive, engaging, learner-centered environment.

We talk about focusing on the "whole child," but do we really address the emotional and psychological needs of our students? Do we venture into the heart of teaching by first crossing the bridge that may lead you and your students into a new world of self-motivation, self-discipline, personal discovery, and self-direction? Why not take the opportunity and just try some of the following suggestions; you, your students, and even their parents may be surprised by the transformation that occurs once students discover their own voice, skills of which they were not aware, and the power of the will that has perhaps remained dormant. Therefore, even though your school day is filled with schedules and learning requirements, you may want to:

For your students:

- Take time to really get to know your students, what their aspirations for the future are.
- Utilize instructional time to ask, then really listen to what students are telling you either vocally or in silence, what they think and feel about their cognitive abilities.
- Provide emotional as well as academic encouragement and support.
- Provide learning opportunities that will give students an opportunity to discover their multiple intelligences.
- Remind your students, on a daily basis, that they possess a very special gift internally that will help them address any and all obstacles they may encounter.

For yourself:

- Be the person you signed on to be when you became a teacher. You are "The Role Model!" Therefore, you must set the tone for your classroom and your students.
- Share some of yourself with them; talk about your dreams and aspirations, how or why you became a teacher; let them see the "human side" of you.
- Exhibit caring and interest in your students' problems and lives. They are aware that you cannot solve their issues, but it always helps to know someone cares.

As you share your gift of teaching with your students, the following strategies and considerations pull the cognitive, affective, and conative domains together for one purpose: success. The following summarizes ways to build and sustain a productive classroom environment throughout the school year.

One student described the type of classroom that makes her feel like working as one in which she feels she is included and has a reason for being there. As she told me her feelings, she looked around the classroom and with a gentle smile of confidence she said to me, "How nice it is to be included—and to include others. You know, being here—this feels like home."

Create a shared vision and action plan with students.

- Build a commitment to initiate positive and productive change.
- Help students pay attention to how they think and respond to simple and complex problems.
- Explore with students effective ways to process and interpret school and life experiences.
- Facilitate opportunities for students to examine how they see themselves and the world around them.
- Ask colleagues and administrators to share ways in which students can more actively participate in school as a "learning community," if there is a need.
- Share your concern when students demonstrate alienation and estrangement from school, peers, and adults. Inquire among staff and stakeholders ways to help them.
- Build new coalitions and instructional practices. Today's world demands that we act with vision, integrity, and caring for all students.
- Tap into the vast untapped source of knowledge that resides within each learner.
- Stimulate tangible aspirations as students gather the courage to share their vision of themselves in the future.
- Discover new and productive ways to work with an increasing range of complex issues many students find themselves facing today.

As young people seek pathways to personal fulfillment and academic achievement, you will make a significant contribution to their success as you help students understand the value of education and life. They want to succeed, they are like the baby eagles, who want to spread their wings and fly; they are anxious to see and experience what is beyond that next mountain. They understand what their future role in this society will or should be. They are also cognizant of the fact that they cannot accomplish the task of obtaining and managing the essential tools of learning without guidance and wisdom from significant others.

Conation and metaconation are energy. Energy is stronger than fear, stronger than anger, stronger than self-doubt, greater than injustice, powerful beyond any thought or deed that seeks to impoverish the human condition. When organized energy comes together for a defined purpose, a new picture emerges.

This energy is the power throughout time that has changed the course of history itself; how we use knowledge to improve the human condition; how we view and implement new goals in education; ways we address health, medical, environmental issues, advances in psychology, physics, chemistry, biology, breakthrough thinking in philosophy, theology, ethics, leadership, the arts, media, sports, high-tech communications, biodiversity, economics, engineering, political processes, global affairs, law, business and so much more.

In the words of Francis W. Parker, "True education frees the human spirit." Within each of us is the fight to reach and grow, to stretch and change, to deliver something spectacular to ourselves, and the world. Conation is the power within that reaches out and drives change, unleashing the desire to learn. Conation's energy keeps us in touch with what we are capable of as students and seekers of knowledge. It is through the strength of conation and metaconation that we become the change the world seeks to know.

Resource A
Teaching to the Test

A REFLECTION

If teaching *to* test becomes the primordial goal of schools, then the focus on testing justifies the neglect of strengthening the human soul. What are we planting in the fertile soil of our children's lives? What will they remember of our presence in their world? What part of our gift of education will they carry with them to guide them on the journey?

Students' perceptions of themselves are the subjective basis upon which they establish their beliefs and personal aspirations. When needed, help them individually to see themselves as the subject of learning in meaningful and life-building ways. We cannot allow students' ability to *"test well"* alone be the only determinant of who they are or what they will become.

Spoken in a way that many of our students feel—the following reflection symbolizes the work that is before us and our students.

TESTING, TESTING, 1, 2, 3, 4, TESTING

Testing, testing, one, two, three, four, testing.
Long tests . . . short tests . . . easy tests . . . hard tests . . . Testing.
One, two, three, four, testing.
State tests, national tests, SAT, ACT. Am I ready, What's in it for me?

Choosing a high school, a college, where should I go?
Uptown, across town, downstate, in state, out of state? Testing.
Admissions forms, financial aid, counselor says, "fill these out and don't be late." Testing.

Peer pressure is on. I don't want to go wrong.
Violence in the streets, morals at stake, decisions to make.
Alcohol's there, drugs everywhere, parents won't listen!
They always say no! What should I do? Where can I go? Testing!
What do I want? Where am I going? Why is life always testing?

Anyone can test me and then criticize. But who will accept me and help me grow from deep inside . . . gaining wisdom so I can be free to actualize dreams and move through life responsibly?
Does anyone hear me?
Testing! Testing! Testing!

Resource B
Your Conative Profile

What is your conative profile? Who's in charge of your life? How strong is your will? To aid in determining the degree in which you engage your *will* in goal attainment, this instrument will assist you in identifying areas of conative strengths and conative needs.

There are two sections to the profile. Read each item in each section and circle the number that best represents your answer. Upon completion of each section, add the numbers that represent your responses. Place your subtotal at the end of each section. Upon completion of the profile, add subtotals of both sections to get your total score.

Section 1

Please rate statements 1–13 as follows: 5 = strongly agree; 4 = agree; 3 = undecided; 2 = disagree; and 1 = strongly disagree.

1. You remain focused on your goals at all times 5 4 3 2 1

2. You believe in yourself. 5 4 3 2 1

3. You believe that you can achieve anything you set out to do 5 4 3 2 1

4. You are a risk taker 5 4 3 2 1

5. You feel that there is room for improvement within yourself 5 4 3 2 1

6. You believe tfiat when necessary, going against the odds is important 5 4 3 2 1

7. You attempt to do your best at all times 5 4 3 2 1

8. You continue to work toward your goal after being told that
    the task is impossible 5 4 3 2 1

9. You put on a take-charge spirit ("I can, I will, I must") and then act
    upon your beliefs 5 4 3 2 1

(Continued)

Your Conative Profile (Continued)

10. When you know you have made the right decision, you act upon your beliefs, even when others' beliefs are distinctly different from yours 5 4 3 2 1

11. You find yourself accomplishing tasks that others might not try 5 4 3 2 1

12. You find yourself turning stumbling blocks into stepping stones..........5 4 3 2 1

13. You tend to focus on what you want in life and go after it with all of your mental and physical energy 5 4 3 2 1

Section 1 Subtotal .... _____

Section 2

Please rate statements 14–20 as follows: 1 = strongly agree; 2 = agree; 3 = undecided; 4 = disagree; 5 = strongly disagree. **Be Careful! The rating system is opposite from the rating system used for the statements in Section 1**

14. You feel that you become a weaker person when you are criticized for your beliefs 1 2 3 4 5

15. You believe that there is simply nothing that you can do to improve your present situation..1 2 3 4 5

16. You generally want others to take on leadership responsibilities, because you feel they probably know more than you do.................1 2 3 4 5

17. You feel that your ideas are not important; therefore, you dismiss them 1 2 3 4 5

18. You find that you spend most of your time just trying to "get by"...........1 2 3 4 5

19. You try to maintain the status quo (i.e., "Good enough is good enough") 1 2 3 4 5

20. You find yourself immobilized when others don't agree with your opinions ...1 2 3 4 5

Section 2 Subtotal .... _____

Total For Section 1 + Section 2 Score: .... _____

Scoring

Remember, as you strengthen your locus of control, personal beliefs, knowledge, skills, and determination, you develop personal tools you can use to change the direction of your learning and your life. Learning and life are personal experiences, requiring personal engagement and lifelong initiatives and commitments.

89–100 Great! You're in the driver's seat. Enjoy the journey while empowering others to join you along the way.

76–88 Awaken your take-charge spirit. Take charge of your learning and your life. Create new experiences for yourself that will allow you to explore life to its fullest. Stretch and grow from your triumphs and your challenges.

0–75 You need a lift. Lifts are good; we all need them. They give us a better view of ourselves and the world. Discover ways to find a more positive sense of self and perspective of life. What do you want to do with your life? What are your goals? Take charge and make changes where needed. Shift your paradigm and experience more joy, success, and personal fulfillment in life and in learning. Become the experience you've been looking for. Express your ability to be remarkable. Choose more than near life experiences. Do something amazing. This is your time. This is your turn. This is your life—Lift it up—Go for it!

References

Albers, P. (2007). *Finding the artist within.* Newark, DE: International Reading Association.

Allee, V. (1997). *The knowledge evolution.* Newton, MA: Butterworth-Heinemann.

Allers, R., & Minkoff, R. (Directors). (1994). *The Lion King.* United States: Walt Disney Pictures.

Allington, R. L., & Cunningham, P. M. (2002). *Schools that work: Where all children read and write* (2nd ed.). Boston: Allyn & Bacon.

Alpert, R., & Haber, R. (1960). Anxiety in academic achievement situations. *Journal of Abnormal and Social Psychology, 61,* 207–215.

American Heritage® Dictionary of the English Language (4th ed.). (2000). Conation. Boston: Houghton Mifflin.

Ames, C. (1992). Classrooms: Goals, structures, and student motivation. *Journal of Educational Psychology, 84,* 261–271.

Ames, C., & Ames, R. (1984). Systems of student and teacher motivation: Toward a qualitative definition. *Journal of Educational Psychology, 76,* 535.

Ames, C., & Archer, J. (1988). Achievement goals in the classroom: Students' learning strategies and motivation processes. *Journal of Educational Psychology, 80,* 260–267.

Amrein, A. L., & Berliner, D. C. (2003). The effects of high-stakes testing on student motivation and learning. *Educational Leadership, 60*(5), 32–37.

Anderman, E. M., & Midgley, C. (1996, March). *Changes in achievement goal orientations after the transition to middle school.* Paper presented at the Biennial Meeting of the Society for Research on Adolescence, Boston, MA. (ERIC Document Reproduction Service No. ED396226)

Annarella, L. (2001). Goal setting: An important part of teaching. *Educational Horizons Archives.* Retrieved October 7, 2003 from http://www.pilambda.org/horizons/v79-2/annarella.pdf.

Armstrong, T. (1994). *Multiple intelligences in the classroom.* Alexandria, VA: Association for Supervision and Curriculum Development.

Armstrong, T. (1998). *Awakening genius in the classroom.* Alexandria, VA: Association for Supervision and Curriculum Development.

Arnold, K. D. (1995). *Lives of promise: What becomes of high school valedictorians: A fourteen-year study of achievement and life choices.* San Francisco: Jossey-Bass.

Assagioli, R. (1973). *The act of the will.* New York: Viking.

Atkinson, J. W., & Birch, D. (1978). *An introduction to motivation* (Rev. ed.). New York: Van Nostrand.

Atkinson, J. W., & Feather, N. T. (1966). *A theory of achievement motivation.* New York: Wiley.

Bagley, C., & Hunter, B. (1992). Constructivism and technology: Forging a new relationship. *Educational Technology, 32*(7), 22–27.

Bagozzi, R. (1992). The self-regulation of attitudes, intentions, and behavior. *Social Psychology Quarterly, 55*(2), 178–204.

Bandura, A. (1977). Self-efficacy: Toward a unifying theory of behavioral change. *Psychological Review, 84*(2), 191–215.

Bandura, A. (1997). *Self-efficacy: The exercise of control.* New York: W. H. Freeman.

Banks, J. A. (1988). Ethnicity, class, cognitive, and motivational styles: Research and teaching implications. *Journal of Negro Education, 57*(4), 452–466.

Barell, J. (1995). *Critical issue: Working toward student self-direction and personal efficacy as educational goals.* Oak Brook, IL: North Central Regional Educational Laboratory. Retrieved October 7, 2003 from http://www.ncrel.org/ncrel/sdrs/areas/issues/students/learning/lr200.htm.

Barr, R., & Parrett, W. (2003). *Saving our students, Saving our schools: 50 proven strategies for revitalizing at-risk students and low-performing schools.* Thousand Oaks, CA: Corwin Press.

Barrett, B. (1931). *Strength of will and how to develop it.* New York: Ruland B. Smith.

Baumeister, R., Bratslavsky, E., Muraven, M., & Tice, D. (1998). Ego depletion: Is the active self a limited resource? *Journal of Personality and Social Psychology, 74*(5), 1252–1265.

Beatty, M., Forst, C., & Stewart, R. (1986). Communication apprehension and motivation as predictors of public speaking duration. *Communication Education, 35*(2), 143–146.

Bellanca, J. (2007). *A guide to graphic organizers: Helping students organize and process content for deeper learning, second edition.* Thousand Oaks, CA: Corwin.

Berendt, P. R., & Koski, B. (1999). No shortcuts to success. *Educational Leadership, 56*(6), 45–47.

Blachowicz, C., & Ogle, D. (2001). *Reading comprehension: Strategies for independent learners.* New York: Guilford Press.

Bloom, B. S., Engelhart, M. D., Furst, E. J., Hill, W. H., & Kratwohl, D. R. (1956). *Taxonomy of educational objectives: The classification of educational goals, By a committee of college and university examiners.* New York: Longmans, Green.

Blumenfeld, P. C. (1992). Classroom learning and motivation: Clarifying and expanding goal theory. *Journal of Educational Psychology, 84*(3), 272–281.

Boethel, M., & Dimock, V. (1999). *Constructing knowledge with technology: A review of the literature.* Austin, TX: Southwest Educational Development Laboratory.

Bohlin, K. E. (Ed.). (2000). Can virtue be taught in the university? *Journal of Education, 182*(2).

Bonwell, C. C., & Eison, J. A. (1991). *Active learning: Creating excitement in the classroom.* (ASHE-ERIC Higher Education Report No. 1). Washington, DC: George Washington University.

Borich, G. D. (2000). *Effective teaching methods* (4th ed.). Upper Saddle River, NJ: Merrill.

Borkowski, J. G., Estrada, M. T., Milstead, M., & Hale, C. A. (1989). General problem-solving skills: Relations between metacognition and strategic processing. *Learning Disability Quarterly, 12*(1), 57–70.

Bransford, J. D., Brown, A. L., & Cocking, R. R. (1999). *How people learn: Brain, mind, experience, and school* (Committee on Developments in the Science of Learning, Commission on Behavioral and Social Sciences and Education, National Research Council). Washington, DC: National Academy Press.

Brooks, J. G., & Brooks, M. G. (1993). *In search of understanding: The case for constructivist classrooms.* Alexandria, VA: Association for Supervision and Curriculum Development.

Brophy, J. (1987). Synthesis of research on strategies for motivating students to learn. *Educational Leadership, 45*(2), 40–48.

Brown, D. A. (1970). *Bury my heart at Wounded Knee: An Indian history of the American West.* New York: Holt, Rinehart & Winston.

Bruner, J. (1996). *The culture of education.* Cambridge, MA: Harvard University.

Brunstein, J., & Gollwitzer, P. (1996). Effects of failure on subsequent performance: The importance of self-defining goals. *Journal of Personality and Social Psychology, 70*, 395–407.

Bryk, A., & Schneider, B (2003). Trust in schools: A core resource for school reform. *Educational Leadership, 6*(6), 40–44.

Buck, R. (1999). The biology of affects: A typology. *Psychological Review, 106*, 301–336.

Bulter, G., & Hope, T. (1995). *Managing your mind: The mental fitness guide.* New York: Oxford University.

Burke, K. (2008). *What to do with the kid who . . . : Developing cooperation, self-discipline, and responsibility in the classroom, third edition.* Thousand Oaks, CA: Corwin.

Buscaglia, L. (1983). *Living, loving, and learning.* New York: Fawcett Columbine.

Cacioppo, J. T., & Petty, R. E. (1982). The need for cognition. *Journal of Personality and Social Psychology, 42*, 116–131.

Caine, R., & Caine, G. (1994). *Making connections: Teaching and the human brain.* Menlo Park, CA: Addison-Wesley.

Campbell, L., & Campbell, B. (1999). *Multiple intelligences and student achievement.* Alexandria, VA: Association for Supervision and Curriculum Development.

Canfield, J., & Wells, H. C. (1994). *100 ways to enhance self-concept in the classroom: A handbook for teachers, counselors, and group leaders* (2nd ed.). Boston: Prentice Hall.

Cassidy, T., & Lynn, R. (1989). A multifactorial approach to achievement motivation: The development of a comprehensive measure. *Journal of Occupational Psychology, 62*, 301–312.

Cawelti, G. (Ed.). (1999). *Handbook of research on improving student achievement* (2nd ed.). Arlington, VA: Educational Research Service.

Classroom Connect. (1997). *Internet curriculum planning system.* Lancaster, PA: Author.

Cohen, D. K., McLaughlin, M. L. W., & Talbert, J. E. (1993). *Teaching for understanding: Challenges for policy and practice.* San Francisco: Jossey-Bass.

Coles, R. (1997). *The moral intelligence of children.* New York: Random.

Collins, D. (1997). *Achieving your vision of professional development: How to assess your needs and get what you want.* Greensboro, NC: SouthEastern Regional Vision for Education (SERVE).

Cooke, G. (2006). *Keys to success for urban school principals, second edition.* Thousand Oaks, CA: Corwin.

Corno, L. (1986). The metacognitive control components of self-regulated learning. *Contemporary Educational Psychology, 11*(4), 333–346.

Corno, L. (1989). Self-regulated learning: A volitional analysis. In B. J. Zimmerman & D. H. Schunk (Eds.), *Self-regulated learning and academic achievement: Theory, research, and practice* (pp. 111–142). New York: Springer-Verlag.

Corno, L. (1992). Encouraging students to take responsibility for learning and performance. *Elementary School Journal, 93*(1), 69–83.

Corno, L., & Kanfer, R. (1993). The role of volition in learning and performance. *Review of Research in Education, 19*, 301–341.

Covey, S. (1990). *Seven habits of highly effective people.* New York: Simon & Schuster.

Crandall, V. C., Katkovsky, W., & Crandall, V. J. (1965). Childrens' beliefs in their own control of reinforcement in intellectual-academic situations. *Child Development, 36*, 91–109.

Crawford, G. (2007). *Brain-based teaching with adolescent learning in mind, Second edition.* Thousand Oaks, CA: Corwin.

Cronbach, L. J. (1990). *Essentials of psychological testing.* New York: Harper & Row.

Csikszentmihalyi, M. (1990). *Flow: The psychology of optimal experience.* New York: Harper & Row.

Curry, L. (1990). *Learning styles in secondary schools: A review of instruments and implications for their use.* Madison: University of Wisconsin, Center for Effective Secondary Schools.

Damon, W. (1999, August). The moral development of children. *Scientific American, 281*, 72–78.

Damon, W. (Ed.). (2002). *Bringing in a new era in character education.* Stanford, CA: Hoover Institution.

Danielson, C. (1996). *Enhancing professional practice: A framework for teaching.* Alexandria, VA: Association for Supervision and Curriculum Development.

Danielson, C. (2002). *Enhancing student achievement: A framework for school improvement.* Alexandria, VA: Association for Supervision and Curriculum Development.

DeBlois, R., & Place, P. (2007). Alternatives for struggling learners. *Principal Leadership. National Association of Secondary School Principals, 7*(8), 38–42.

Deci, E. L., & Ryan, R. M. (1985). *Intrinsic motivation and self determination in human behavior.* New York: Plenum.

Deiro, J. (1996). *Teaching with heart: Making healthy connections with students.* Thousand Oaks, CA: Corwin.

Dennett, D. C. (1978). Skinner skinned. In D. C. Dennett, *Brainstorms: Philosophical essays on mind and psychology* (pp. 53–70). Cambridge, MA: Bradford.

Dewey, J. (1933). *How we think.* Boston: D. C. Heath.

Diener, C. I., & Dweck, C. S. (1978). An analysis of learned helplessness: Continuous changes in performance, strategy, and achievement cognitions following failure. *Journal of Personality and Social Psychology, 36*(5), 451–462.

Diener, C. I., & Dweck, C. S. (1980). An analysis of learned helplessness II: The processing of success. *Journal of Personality and Social Psychology, 47*, 580–592.

Dole, J. A., Duffy, G. G., Roehler, L. R., & Pearson, P. D. (1991). Moving from the old to the new: Research on reading comprehension instruction. *Review of Educational Research, 61*(2), 239–264.

Domino, G. (1968). Differential predictions of academic achievement in conforming and independent settings. *Journal of Educational Psychology, 59*, 256–260.

Domino, G. (1971). Interactive effects of achievement orientation and teaching style on academic achievement. *Journal of Educational Psychology, 62*, 427–431.

Donagan, A. (1987). *Choice, The essential element in human action.* London: Routledge Kegan Paul.

Dretske, F. (1981). *Knowledge and the flow of information.* Cambridge, MA: Massachusetts Institute of Technology.

Druva, C., & Anderson, R. D. (1983). Science teacher characteristics by teacher behavior and by student outcome: A meta-analysis of research. *Journal of Research in Science Teaching, 20*(5), 467–479.

Dunn, R., & Dunn, K. (1978). *Teaching students through their individual learning styles: A practical approach.* Reston, VA: Reston Publishing.

Dweck, C. S. (1986). Motivational processes affecting learning. *American Psychologist, 41*(10), 1040–1048.

Dweck, C. S., & Leggett, E. L. (1988). A social-cognitive approach to motivation and personality. *Psychological Review 95*(2), 256–273.

Edmonds, R. (1979). Effective schools for the urban poor. *Educational Leadership, 37*(1), 15–18, 20–24.

Edwards, P., Pleasants, H. M., & Franklin, S. H. (1999). *A path to follow: Listen to parents.* Portsmouth, NH: Heinemann.

Eisner, E. W. (1991). What really counts in schools. *Educational Leadership, 48*(5), 10–11, 14–17.

Elias, M. J., Zins, J. E., Weissberg, R. P., Frey, K. S., Greenberg, M. T., Haynes, N. M., Kessler, R., Schwab-Stone, M.E., & Shriver, T. P. (1997). *Promoting social and emotional learning: Guidelines for educators.* Alexandria, VA: Association for Supervision and Curriculum Development.

Elliott, P. (1986). Right (or left) brain cognition, wrong metaphor for creative behavior: It is prefrontal lobe volition that makes the difference in the release of creative potential. *Journal of Creative Behavior, 20*(3), 202–214.

Elliott, E. S., & Dweck, C. S. (1988). Goals: An approach to motivation and achievement. *Journal of Personality and Social Psychology, 54*, 5–12.

Ellis, A. K., & Fouts, J. T. (1997). *Research on educational innovations.* Larchmont, NY: Eye on Education.

Ellsworth, J. H. (1994). *Education on the Internet.* Indianapolis: Sams.

Ely, D. P., et al. (1996). *Trends in educational technology 1995.* Syracuse, NY: Information Resources Publications, Syracuse University. (ERIC Document Reproduction Service No. ED396717)

Emmons, R. (1986). Personal strivings: An approach to personality and subjective well-being. *Journal of Personality and Social Psychology, 51*, 1058–1068.

English, H., & English, A. (1958). *A comprehensive dictionary of psychological and psychoanalytical terms.* New York: Longmans, Green.

Entwistle, N. (1987b). *Understanding classroom learning.* London: Hodder and Stoughton.

Entwistle, N., & Ramsden, P. (1983). *Understanding student learning.* London: Groom Helm.

Epstein, J. L. (1995). School/family/community partnerships: Caring for the children we share. *Phi Delta Kappan, 76*(9), 701–712.

Epstein, J. L. (2001). *School, family, and community partnerships: Preparing educators and improving schools.* Boulder, CO: Westview.

Epstein, S. (1990). Cognitive-experiential self-theory. In L. A. Pervin (Ed.), *Handbook of personality: Theory and research* (pp. 165–191). New York: Guilford.

Erickson, E. (1968). *Identity: Youth in crisis.* New York: W. W. Norton.

Erickson, L. H. (2007). *Stirring the head, heart, and soul: Redefining curriculum, instruction, and concept-based learning, third edition.* Thousand Oaks, CA: Corwin.

Eysenck, H. J., & Eysenck, M. W. (1985). *Personality and individual differences.* New York: Plenum.

Fennimore, T. F., & Tinzmann, M. B. (1990). *What is a thinking curriculum?* Oak Brook, IL: North Central Regional Educational Laboratory. Retrieved October 7, 2003 from http://www.ncrel.org/sdrs/areas/rpl_esys/thinking.htm.

Festinger, L. (1957). *A theory of cognitive dissonance.* Evanston, IL: Row, Peterson.

Fetler, M. (1999). High school staff characteristics and mathematics test results. *Educational Policy Analysis Archives, 7*(9). (ERIC Document Reproduction Service No. EJ588920)

Fineman, S. (1977). The achievement motive construct and its measurement: Where are we now? *British Journal of Psychology, 68*, 1–22.

Ford, E., & Ford, D. H. (1987). *Humans as self-constructing living systems.* Hillsdale, NJ: Lawrence Erlbaum.

Fosnot, C. (1992). Constructing constructivism. In T. Duffy & D. Jonassen (Eds.), *Constructivism and the technology of instruction, A conversation* (pp. 167–176). Hillsdale, NJ: Lawrence Erlbaum.

Foucault, M. (1988). Technologies of the self. In L. Martin, H. Gutman, & P. Hutton (Eds.), *Technologies of the self* (pp. 16–49). Amherst: University of Massachusetts.

Fowler, C. (1989). The arts are essential to education. *Educational Leadership, 47*(3), 60–63.

Frank, A. (1956). *Anne Frank: The diary of a young girl.* (Translated by B. M. Moojart-Doubleday). New York: Random House.

Frankfurt, H. (1982). Freedom of the will and the concept of a person. In G. Watson (Ed.), *Free will* (pp. 96–110). Oxford: Oxford University.

Frankl, V. (1998). *Man's search for meaning* (Rev. ed.). New York: Washington Square.

Freeman, R. (1991). *The Wright brothers: How they invented the airplane.* New York: Holiday House.

Fried, R. L. (2001). *The passionate learner . . . How teachers and parents can help children reclaim the joy of discovery.* Boston: Beacon Press.

Frymier, A. B., & Shulman, G. (1995). What's in it for me?: Increasing content relevance to enhance students' motivation. *Communication Education, 44*(1), 40–50.

Fullan, M. (1993). *Change forces.* New York: Falmer.

Gaines, S. O., Jr., Panter, A. T., Lyde, M. D., Steers, W. N., Rusbult, C. E., Cox, C. L., & Wexler, M. O. (1997). Evaluating the circumplexity of interpersonal traits and the manifestation of interpersonal traits in interpersonal trust. *Journal of Personality and Social Psychology, 73*, 610–623.

Gardner, H. (1989). Beyond a modular view of mind. In W. Damon (Ed.), *Child development today and tomorrow* (pp. 222 –239). San Francisco: Jossey-Bass.

Gardner, H. (1993). *Frames of mind: The theory of multiple intelligences* (10th anniversary ed.). New York: Basic Books.

Garmezy, N. (1991). Resiliency and vulnerability to adverse developmental outcomes associated with poverty. *American Behavioral Scientist, 34*(4), 416–430.

Gelzheiser, L., & d'Angelo, C. (2000). Historical fiction and informational texts that support social studies standards: An annotated bibliography. *The Language and Literacy Spectrum, 10,* 26–39.

Gholar, C., Givens, S., McPherson, M., & Riggs, E. (1991, April). *Wellness begins when the child comes first: The relationship between the conative domain and the school achievement paradigm.* Paper presented at the annual convention of the American Association for Counseling and Development, Reno, NV.

Gholar, C. R., & Riggs, E. G. (2004). *Connecting with students' will to succeed: The power of conation* (1st ed.). Thousand Oaks, CA: Corwin Press.

Giroux, H. A. (1988). *Teachers as intellectuals: Toward a critical pedagogy of learning.* Granby, MA: Bergin and Garvey.

Glasser, W. (2000). *Every child can succeed.* Chula Vista, CA: Black Forest Press.

Glasser, W. (1990). *The quality school: Managing students without coercion.* New York: Perennial Library.

Godfrey, R. (1992). Civilization, education, and the visual arts: A personal manifesto. *Phi Delta Kappan, 73*(8), 596–598, 600.

Goldschmidt, P., & Wang, J. (1999). When can schools affect dropout behavior? A longitudinal multilevel analysis. *American Educational Research Journal, 36*(4), 715–738.

Goleman, D. (1995). *Emotional intelligence: Why it can matter more than IQ for character, health and lifelong achievement.* New York: Bantam.

Gollwitzer, P. (1996). Action phases and mind-sets. In E. Higgins & R. Sorrentino (Eds.), *Handbook of motivation and cognition, Vol. 2* (pp. 53–92). New York: Guilford.

Goodlad, J. L. (1984). *A place called school: Prospects for the future.* New York: McGraw-Hill.

Goodlad, J. L. (1994). *Educational renewal: Better teachers, better schools.* San Francisco: Jossey-Bass.

Goodnow, J. J. (1980). Everyday concepts of intelligence and its development. In N. Warren (Ed.), *Studies in cross-cultural psychology, Vol. 2* (pp. 191–219). Oxford: Pergamon.

Gottfried, J., & McFeely, M. G. (1997). Learning all over the place: Integrating laptop computers into the classroom. *Learning and Leading with Technology, 25*(4), 6–11.

Grasha, A. F. (1996). *Teaching with style: A practical guide to enhancing learning by understanding teaching and learning styles.* Pittsburgh, PA: Alliance.

Griggs, S. A. (1991). *Learning styles counseling.* Ann Arbor, MI: University of Michigan, ERIC Counseling and Personnel Services.

Gunning, T. (2000). *Creating literacy instruction for all children.* Boston: Allyn & Bacon.

Guthrie, J. T., Wigfield, A., & VonSecker, C. (2000). Effects of integrated instruction on motivation and strategy use in reading. *Journal of Educational Psychology, 92*(2), 331–341.

Haines, J. (1996). *Stories without endings: Ash-Shadid—"The Witness."* Upper Saddle River, NJ: Globe Fearon.

Hale-Benson, J. E. (1986). *Black children: Their roots, culture, and learning styles* (Rev. ed.). Baltimore, MD: Johns Hopkins University.

Hargreaves, A. (1994). *Changing teachers, changing times.* New York: Teachers College Press.

Harlan, J. C., & Rowland, S. T. (2002). *Behavior management strategies for teachers: Achieving instructional effectiveness, student success, and student motivation—Every teacher and any student can!* (2nd ed.). Springfield, IL: Charles C Thomas.

Harmin, M. (1995). *Strategies to inspire active learning.* Edwardsville, IL: Inspiring Strategy Institute.

Harter, S. (1981). A new self-report scale of intrinsic vs. extrinsic orientation in the classroom: Motivational and informational components. *Developmental Psychology, 17,* 300–312.

Harter, S., & Connell, J. P. (1984). A model of children's achievement and related self-perceptions of competence, control, and motivational orientation. *Advances in Motivation and Achievement, 3,* 219–250.

Haycock, K. (1998). *Good teaching matters.* Washington, DC: Education Trust.

Healy, J. (1994). *Your child's growing mind: A guide to learning and brain development from birth to adolescence* (New ed.). New York: Doubleday.

Healy, J. (1999). *Endangered minds: Why children don't think—And what we can do about it.* New York: Simon & Schuster.

Heckhausen, H. (1967). *The anatomy of achievement motivation.* New York: Academic.

Heckhausen, H. (1977). Achievement motivation and its constructs: A cognitive model. *Motivation and Emotion, 1,* 283–329.

Heckhausen, H., & Kuhl, J. (1985). From wishes to action: The dead ends and shortcuts on the long way to action. In M. Frese & J. Sarini (Eds.), *Goal-directed behavior: Psychological theory and research on action* (pp. 134–159). Hillsdale, NJ: Lawrence Erlbaum.

Heckhausen, H., Schmalt, H. D., & Schneider, K. (1985). *Achievement motivation in perspective.* Orlando, FL: Academic.

Heckhausen, J., & Dweck, C. (Eds.). (1998). *Motivation and self-regulation across the life span.* New York: Cambridge University Press.

Hehir, T. (2005). The changing role of intervention for children with disabilities. *Principal Leadership National Association of Secondary School Principals. 85*(2), 22-25.

Hembree, R. (1988). Correlates, causes, effects, and treatment of test anxiety. *Review of Educational Research, 58*(1), 47–77.

Hershberger, W. (1987). Of course there can be an empirical science of volitional action. *American Psychologist, 42,* 1032–1033.

Hershberger, W. (1988). Psychology as a conative science. *American Psychologist, 43*(10), 823–824.

Hershberger, W. (Ed.). (1989). *Volitional action: Conation and control.* Amsterdam: Elsevier Science.

Higgins, E. T. (1987). Self-discrepancy: A theory relating self and affect. *Psychological Review, 94,* 319–340.

Hilgard, E. R. (1980). The trilogy of mind: Cognition, affection, and conation. *Journal of the History of Behavioral Sciences, 16,* 107–117.

Hilliard, Asa, III. (1991). Do we have the will to educate all children? *Educational Leadership, 49*(1), 31–36.

Hixson, J., Gholar, C., & Riggs, E. (1999). *Ensuring success for "low yield" students: Building lives and molding futures.* Retrieved October 7, 2003 from http://www.teachstream.com.

Ho, D. (1995). Internalized culture, culturocentrism, and transcendance. *Counseling Psychologist, 23*(1), 4–24.

Hoerr, T. R. (1996). Collegiality: A new way to define instructional leadership. *Phi Delta Kappan, 77*(5), 380–381.

Hom, H. L., Jr., & Murphy, M. D. (1983). Low achiever's performance: The positive impact of a self-directed goal. *Personality and Social Psychology Bulletin, 11,* 275–285.

Howe, M. J. A., Davidson, J. W., & Sloboda, J. A. (1998). Innate talents: Reality or myth? *Behavioral and Brain Sciences, 21,* 399–442.

Huitt, W. (1995/1999). *Success in the information age: A paradigm shift.* Valdosta, GA: Valdosta State University. Retrieved October 7, 2003 from http://chiron.valdosta.edu/whuitt/col/context/infoage.html.

Huitt, W. (1999). *Conation as an important factor of mind.* Retrieved October 7, 2003 from http://chiron.valdosta.edu/whuitt/col/regsys/conation.html.

Hunsley, J. (1987). Cognitive processes in mathematics anxiety and test anxiety: The role of appraisals, internal dialogue, and attributions. *Journal of Educational Psychology, 79,* 388–392.

Hutchinson encyclopedia. (2000). Conation. Oxford: Helicon.

Hyerle, D. (1996). *Visual tools for constructing knowledge.* Alexandria, VA: Association for Supervision and Curriculum Development.

Intrator, S.M, (2006). Starting with the soul. *Educational Leadership, 63*(6), 38–40.

Izard, C. E. (1992). Basic emotions, relations among emotions, and emotion-cognition relations. *Psychological Review, 99,* 561–565.

Izard, C. E., Kagan, J., & Zajonc, R. B. (Eds.). (1984). *Emotions, cognition, and behavior.* New York: Cambridge University Press.

Izumi, L. T., & Evers, W. M. (Eds.). (2002). *Teacher quality.* San Francisco: Pacific Research Institute.

Jackson, D. N., Ahmed, S. A., & Heapy, N. A. (1976). Is achievement a unitary construct? *Journal of Research in Personality, 10,* 1–21.

Jensen, E. (1995). *Superteaching: Success strategies that bring out the best in both you and your students.* Del Mar, CA: Turning Point.

Jensen, E. (1998). *Teaching with the brain in mind.* Alexandria, VA: Association for Supervision and Curriculum Development.

Jewett, J., & Katzev, A. (1993). *School-based early childhood centers: Secrets of success from early innovators.* Portland, OR: Child, Family, and Community Program, Northwest Regional Educational Laboratory.

Johnson-Laird, P. N., & Oatley, K. (1992). Basic emotions, rationality, and folk theory. *Cognition and Emotion, 6,* 201–223.

Jones, B., Valdez, G., Nowakowski, J., & Rasmussen, C. (1995). Table 1: Indicators of engaged learning. In *Plugging In: Choosing and Using Educational Technology.* Naperville, IL: North Central Regional Educational Laboratory. Retrieved October 7, 2003 from http://www.ncrel.org/sdrs/edtalk/toc.htm.

Jones, B. F., Palincsar, A. S., Ogle, D. S., & Carr, E. G. (1987). *Strategic teaching and learning: Cognitive instruction in the content areas.* Alexandria, VA: Association for Supervision and Curriculum Development.

Jones, E. N., Ryan, K., & Bohlin, K. E. (1999). *Teachers as educators of character: Are the nation's schools of education coming up short?* Washington, DC; Boston, MA: Character Education Partnership; Boston University's Center for the Advancement of Ethics and Character.

Joyce, B. R., & Calhoun, E. F. (1996). *Creating learning experiences: The role of instructional theory and research.* Alexandria, VA: Association for Supervision and Curriculum Development.

Kavanaugh, D., & Bower, G. (1985). Mood and self-efficacy: Impact of job and sadness on perceived capabilities. *Cognitive Therapy and Research, 9,* 507–525.

Keefe, J. W. (1979). Learning style: An overview. In *Student learning styles: Diagnosing and prescribing programs* (pp. 1–17). Reston, VA: National Association of Secondary School Principals.

Keefe, J. W. (1987). *Learning style theory and practice.* Reston, VA: National Association of Secondary School Principals.

Keller, H. (2003). *The story of my life* (with supplementary accounts by A. Sullivan & J. A. Macy; edited by R. Shattuck with D. Herrmann). New York: Norton.

Kessler, R. (2000). *The soul of education.* Alexandria, VA: Association for Supervision and Curriculum Development.

Kim, R., & Hwan, M. (2002). The effect of Internal control and achievement motivation in group counseling based on reality therapy. *International Journal of Reality Therapy.*

Kline, P. (1973). *New approaches in psychological measurement.* New York: Wiley.

Kline, P., & Cooper, C. (1984). A construct validation of the Objective-Analytic Test Battery (OATB). *Personality and Individual Differences, 5,* 323–337.

Kohl, H. (1991). *I won't learn from you!: The role of assent in learning.* Minneapolis: Milkweed.

Kohn, A. (1993). *Punished by rewards: The trouble with gold stars, incentive plans, A's, praise, and other bribes.* Boston: Houghton Mifflin.

Kolb, D. A. (1984). *Experiential learning: Experience as the source of learning and development.* Englewood Cliffs, NJ: Prentice Hall.

Kolbe, K. (1990). *The conative connection.* Reading, MA: Addison-Wesley.

Kozol, J. (1991). *Savage inequalities: Children in America's schools.* New York: Crown.

Kroeger, O., & Thuesen, J. (1988). *Type talk: The 16 personality types that determine how we live, love, and work.* New York: Dell.

Kuhl, J. (1981). Motivational and functional helplessness: The moderating effect of state versus action orientation. *Journal of Personality and Social Psychology, 40,* 155–170.

Kuhl, J. (1984). Volitional aspects of achievement motivation and learned helplessness: Toward a comprehensive theory of action control. In B. A. Maher (Ed.), *Progress in experimental personality research, Vol. 12* (pp. 99–170). New York: Academic.

Kuhl, J. (1987). Feeling versus being helpless: Metacognitive mediation of failure-induced performance deficits. In F. Weinert & R. Kluwe (Eds.), *Metacognition, motivation, and understanding* (pp. 217–235). Hillsdale, NJ: Lawrence Erlbaum.

Kuhl, J., & Beckmann, J. (Eds.). (1985). *Action control, from cognition to behavior.* New York: Springer-Verlag.

Kuhl, J., & Beckmann, J. (Eds.) (1994). *Volition and personality: Action versus state orientation.* Seattle: Hogrefe and Huber.

Kuhl, J., & Kraska, K. (1989). Self-regulation and metamotivation: Computational mechanisms, development, and assessment. In R. Kanfer, P. L. Ackerman, & R. Cudeck (Eds.), *Abilities, motivation, and methodology* (pp. 343–374). Hillsdale, NJ: Lawrence Erlbaum.

Ladson-Billings, G. (1995). *The dreamkeepers: Successful teachers of African American children.* San Francisco: Jossey-Bass.

Lafer, S. (1997). Audience, elegance, and learning via the Internet. *Computers in the Schools, 13*(1–2), 89–97.

Lazarus, R. S. (1991). *Emotion and adaptation.* New York: Oxford University Press.

Lebow, D. G., & Wager, W. W. (1994). Authentic activity as a model for appropriate learning activity: Implications for emerging instructional technologies. *Canadian Journal of Educational Communication, 23,* 231–244.

LeDoux, J. (1996). *The emotional brain: The mysterious underpinnings of emotional life.* New York: Simon & Schuster.

Lens, W. (1983). *Achievement motivation, test anxiety, and academic achievement.* Leuven, Belgium: University of Leuven Psychological Reports.

Lens, W., & DeCruyenaere, M. (1991). Motivation and de-motivation in secondary education: Student characteristics. *Learning and Instruction, 1*(2), 145–159.

Leondari, A., Syngollitou, E., & Kiosseoglou, G. (1998). Academic achievement, motivation and future selves. *Educational Studies, 24*(2), 153–163.

Lepper, M. R. (1988). Motivational considerations in the study of instruction. *Cognition and Instruction, 5,* 289–310.

Lewis, C., Schaps, E., & Watson, M. (1995). Beyond the pendulum: Creating challenging and daring schools. *Phi Delta Kappan, 76*(7), 547–554.

Lieberman, A. (1995). Practices that support teacher development: Transforming conceptions of professional learning. *Phi Delta Kappan, 76*(8), 591–596.

Liebert, R., & Morris, L. (1967). Cognitive and emotional components of test anxiety: A distinction and some initial data. *Psychological Reports, 20,* 975–978.

Lispsitz, J. (1977). *Growing up forgotten: A review of research and programs concerning early adolescence: A report to the Ford Foundation.* Lexington, MA: Lexington Books.

Lounsbury, J. H. (1996). Key characteristics of middle level schools. *ERIC Digest.* (ERIC Document Reproduction Service No. ED401050)

Lynn, R., Hampson, S. L., & Magee, M. (1983). Determinants of educational achievement at 16+: Intelligence, personality, home background, and school. *Personality and Individual Differences, 4,* 473–481.

Malloch, R. D. (1990). *Identification of underlying components of academic awareness.* Unpublished doctoral dissertation, University of Texas at Austin.

Malone, T. W., & Lepper, M. R. (1987). Making learning fun: A taxonomy of intrinsic motivations for learning. In R. E. Snow & M. J. Farr (Eds.), *Aptitude, learning and instruction: Vol. 3. Cognitive and affective process analysis* (pp. 223–253). Hillsdale, NJ: Lawrence Erlbaum.

Mandler, G., & Sarason, S. (1952). A study of anxiety and learning. *Journal of Abnormal and Social Psychology, 47,* 166–173.

Marton, F., Hounsell, D. J., & Entwistle, N. J. (Eds.). (1984). *The experience of learning.* Edinburgh: Scottish Academic Press.

Marton, F., & Saljo, R. (1976). On qualitative differences in learning: I—Outcome and process. *British Journal of Educational Psychology, 46,* 4–11.

Marzano, R. J. (2005). *School leadership that works.* Alexandria, VA: Association for Supervision and Curriculum Development.

Marzano, R. J. (2003). *What works in schools: Transforming research into action.* Alexandria, VA: Association for Supervision and Curriculum Development.

Marzano, R., & Marzano, J. (2003). The key to classroom management. *Educational Leadership, 61*(1), 6–13.

Maslow, A. H. (1987). *Motivation and personality* (3rd ed.). New York: Harper & Row.

McClelland, D. C. (1961). *The achieving society.* Princeton, NJ: Van Nostrand.

McClelland, D. C., Atkinson, J. W., Clark, R. A., & Lowell, E. L. (1953). *The achievement motive.* New York: Appleton-Century-Crofts.

McClelland, D. C., Koestner, R., & Weinberger, J. (1989). How do self-attributed and implicit motives differ? *Psychological Review, 96,* 690–702.

McCombs, B., & Whisler, J. (1989). The role of affective variables in autonomous learning. *Educational Psychologist, 24*(3), 277–306.

McKeachie, W. (1986). *Teaching tips* (8th ed.). Lexington, MA: Heath.

Means, B., & Olson, K. (1994). The link between technology and authentic learning. *Educational Leadership, 51*(7), 15–18.

Mevarech, Z. R., Silber, O., & Fine, D. (1991). Learning with computers in small groups: Cognitive and affective outcomes. *Journal of Educational Computing Research, 7*(2), 233–243.

Miller, A. (1991). Personality types, learning styles, and educational goals. *Educational Psychology, 11*(3–4), 217–238.

Miller, J. P. (2002). *Education and the soul: Toward a spiritual curriculum.* Albany: State University of New York.

Miller, R., Greene, B., Montalvo, G., Ravindran, B., & Nichols, J. (1996). Engagement in academic work: The role of learning goals, future consequences, pleasing others, and perceived ability. *Contemporary Educational Psychology, 21*(4), 388–422.

Mischel, W. (1973). Toward a cognitive social learning reconceptualization of personality. *Psychological Review, 80,* 252–283.

Mischel, W. (1996). From good intentions to willpower. In P. Gollwitzer & J. Bargh (Eds.), *The psychology of action* (pp. 197–218). New York: Guilford.

Mischel, W., & Shoda, Y. (1995). A cognitive-affective system theory of personality: Reconceptualizing situations, dispositions, dynamics, and invariance in personality structure. *Psychological Review, 102*, 246–268.

Moline, S. (1995). *I see what you mean: Children at work with visual information.* York, ME: Stenhouse Publishers.

Morris, H., & Snyder, R. A. (1978). Convergent validities of the Resultant Achievement Motivation Test and the Prestatie Motivatie Test with Ac and Ai scales of the CPI. *Educational and Psychological Measurement, 38*, 1151–1155.

Mueller, C., & Dweck, C. (1998). Praise for intelligence can undermine children's motivation and performance. *Journal of Personality and Social Psychology, 75*(1), 33–52.

Murray, H. A. (1938). *Explorations in personality.* Cambridge, MA: Harvard University.

Myers, I. B. (1980). *Gifts differing.* Palo Alto, CA: Consulting Psychologists.

National Council of Teachers of Mathematics. (1989). *Curriculum and evaluation standards for school mathematics.* Reston, VA: Author.

Naveh-Benjamin, M., McKeachie, W., & Lin, Y. G. (1987). Two types of test anxious students: Support for an information processing model. *Journal of Educational Psychology, 79*, 131–136.

Naveh-Benjamin, M., McKeachie, W., Lin, Y. G., & Tucker, D. G. (1986). Inferring students' cognitive structures and their development using the Ordered Tree Technique. *Journal of Educational Psychology, 78*, 130–140.

Nenniger, P. (1987). How stable is motivation by contents? In E. de Corte, H. Lodwijks, R. Parmentier, & P. Span (Eds.), *Learning and instruction: European research in an international context, Vol. 1* (pp. 159–179). London: Pergamon.

Nicholls, J. G., Cheung, P. C., Lauer, J., & Patashnick, M. (1989). Individual differences in academic motivation: Perceived ability, goals, beliefs, and values. *Learning and Individual Differences, 1*, 63–84.

Nicholls, J. G., & Dweck, C. S. (1979). *A definition of achievement motivation.* Unpublished manuscript, University of Illinois at Champaign-Urbana.

Nicholls, J. G., Patashnick, M., & Nolen, S. B. (1985). Adolescents' theories of education. *Journal of Educational Psychology, 77*(6), 683–692.

Nieto, S. (1994). Lessons from students on creating a chance to dream. *Harvard Educational Review, 64*(4), 392–426.

Nieto, S. (2003). What keeps teachers going? *Educational Leadership, 60*(8), 14–18.

Novick, R. (1996). *School-based early childhood centers: Challenges and possibilities.* Portland, OR: Northwest Regional Educational Laboratory.

Oatley, K., & Johnson-Laird, P. N. (1987). Towards a cognitive theory of emotions. *Cognition and Emotion, 1*, 29–50.

Ogle, D. (2000). Make it visual. In M. McLaughlin & M. Vogt (Eds.), *Creativity and innovation in content area teaching* (pp. 103–114). Norwood, MA: Christopher Gordon.

Oldfather, P. (1995). Commentary: What's needed to maintain and extend motivation for literacy in the middle grades? *Journal of Reading, 38*(6), 420–422.

Olness, R. (2007). *Using literature to enhance content area instruction.* Newark, DE: International Reading Association.

Olsen, J. T. (1974). *Jackie Robinson: Pro ball's first Black star.* (Illustrated by H. Henriksen.) Mankato, MN: Creative Education.

Ormrod, J. E. (2006). *Educational psychology, developing learners* (5th Ed.). Upper Saddle River, NJ: Pearson.

Ormond, W. (2000). *Pacific megatrends in education* (PREL Briefing Paper). Honolulu, HI: Pacific Resources for Education and Learning. (ERIC Document Reproduction Service No. ED446360)

Palmer, P. J. (1998). *The courage to teach.* San Francisco: Jossey-Bass.

Panksepp, J. (1982). Toward a general psychobiological theory of emotions. *The Behavioral and Brain Sciences, 5,* 407–467.

Paris, S. G., & Winograd, P. (1990). How metacognition can promote academic learning and instruction. In B. F. Jones & I. Idol (Eds.), *Dimensions of thinking and cognitive instruction.* Hillsdale, NJ: Lawrence Erlbaum.

Pears, D. (Ed.). (1963). *Freedom and the will.* New York: St. Martin's Press.

Perkins, D. (1992). *Smart schools: From training memories to educating minds.* New York: Free Press.

Perrone, V. (Ed.). (1991). *Expanding student assessment.* Alexandria, VA: Association for Supervision and Curriculum Development.

Pert, C. B. (1997). *Molecules of emotion: Why you feel the way you feel.* New York: Scribner.

Phillip, H. (1936). *An experimental study of the frustration of will—Acts and conation.* Cambridge, England: Cambridge University Press.

Piaget, J. (1929). *The child's conception of the world.* New York: Harcourt Brace.

Piaget, J. (1970). *The place of the sciences of man in the system of sciences.* New York: Harper & Row.

Piaget, J. (1972). *The psychology of intelligence.* Totowa, NJ: Littlefield, Adams.

Pintrich, P. R., McKeachie, W. J., Smith, D. A., Doljanac, R., Lin, Y. G., Naveh-Benjamin, M., Crooks, T., & Karabenick, S. (1988). *Motivated strategies for learning questionnaire.* Ann Arbor: University of Michigan, National Center for Research to Improve Postsecondary Teaching and Learning.

Piper, W. (1991). *The little engine that could* [from the original story by W. Piper; illustrated by C. Ong]. New York: Platt and Munk.

Pitcher, S. M., Albright, L. K., Delaney, C. J., Walker, N. T., Seunarinsesingh, K., Mogge, S., Keadley, K., Ridgeway, V. G., Peck, S., Hunt, R., & Dunston, P. J. (2007). Assessing adolescents' motivation to read. *Journal of Adolescent & Adult Literacy. 50*(5), 378–395.

Prawat, R. (1985). Affective versus cognitive goal orientations in elementary teachers. *American Educational Research Journal, 22*(4), 587–604.

Prenzel, M. (1988, April). *Conditions for the persistence of interest.* Paper presented at the annual meeting of the American Educational Research Association, New Orleans, LA.

Pressley, M. (1987). *What is good strategy use and why is it hard to teach? An optimistic appraisal of the challenges associated with strategy instruction.* Paper presented at annual convention of American Educational Research Association, Washington, DC.

Pressley, M., Wood, E., Woloshyn, V., Martin, V., King, A., & Menke, D. (1992). Encouraging mindful use of prior knowledge: Attempting to construct explanatory answers facilities learning. *Educational Psychologist, 27*(winter), 1.

Proctor, R. W., & Dutta, A. (1995). *Skill acquisition and human performance.* Thousand Oaks, CA: Sage Publications.

Purkey, W. W. (1978). *Inviting school success: A self-concept approach to teaching and learning.* Belmont, CA: Wadsworth.

Purkey, W. W., & Novak, J. M. (1984). *Inviting school success: A self-concept approach to teaching and learning* (2nd ed.). Belmont, CA: Wadsworth.

Purkey, W. W., & Novak, J. M. (1986). *Inviting school success: A self-concept approach to teaching, learning, and democratic practice* (3rd ed.). Belmont, CA: Wadsworth.

Rafaeli-Mor, E., & Steinberg, J. (2002). Self-complexity and well-being: A review and research synthesis. *Personality and Social Psychology Review, 6,* 31–58.

Raffini, J. P. (1996). *150 ways to increase intrinsic motivation in the classroom.* Boston: Allyn & Bacon.

Rand, P., & Others. (1991). Negative motivation is half the story: Achievement motivation combines positive and negative motivation. *Scandinavian Journal of Educational Research, 35*(1), 13–30. (ERIC Document Reproduction Service No. EJ423891)

Ray, J. J. (1982). *Self-report measures of achievement motivation: A catalog.* New South Wales, Australia: University of New South Wales. (ERIC Document Reproduction Service No. ED237523)

Reber, A. S. (1993). *Implicit learning and tacit knowledge: An essay on the cognitive unconscious.* Oxford: Oxford University Press.

Reeves, D. (2000). *Accountability in action.* Denver, CO: Advanced Learning Press.

Reisenzein, R., & Schonpflug, W. (1992). Stumpf's cognitive-evaluative theory of emotion. *American Psychologist, 47,* 34–45.

Reitzug, U. C., & Burrello, L. C. (1995). How principals can build self-renewing schools. *Educational Leadership, 52*(7), 48–50.

Richardson, J., Morgan, R. F, & Fleener, C. (2006). *Reading to learn in the content areas.* Belmont, CA: Thomson Higher Education.

Richmond, V. (1990). Communication in the classroom: Power and motivation. *Communication Education, 39*(3), 181–195.

Ridnoner, K. (2006). *Managing your classroom with heart: A guide for nurturing adolescent learners.* Alexandria, VA: Association for Supervision and Curriculum Development

Riggs, E. G., & Gil-Garcia, A. (2001). *Helping middle and high school readers: Teaching and learning strategies across the curriculum.* Arlington, VA: Educational Research Service.

Robinson, J. P., Shaver, P. R., & Wrightsman, L. S. (1991). *Measures of personality and social psychological attitudes.* San Diego: Academic Press.

Rogat, M. (2005). Kid-to-kid: Guiding our students toward self-confidence and personal power. *Middle Ground, 9*(2), 12-14.

Rogers, T. B. (1973). Ratings of content as a means of assessing personality items. *Educational and Psychological Measurement, 33,* 845–858.

Rollett, B. A. (1987). Effort avoidance and learning. In E. de Corte, H. Lodewijks, & R. Parmentier (Eds.), *Learning and instruction: European research in an international context, Vol. 1* (pp. 147–157). Oxford: Pergamon.

Rosenthal, R., & Jacobson, L. (1968). *Pygmalion in the classroom: Teacher expectation and pupils' intellectual development.* New York: Holt, Rinehart, and Winston.

Rothstein, R., Wilder, T., & Jacobsen, Rebecca. (2007). Balance the balance. *Educational Leadership, 64*(8-14).

Ryan, K., & Bohlin, K. E. (1999). *Building character in schools: Practical ways to bring moral instruction to life.* San Francisco: Jossey-Bass.

Ryan, R. M., & Connell, J. P. (1989). Perceived locus of causality and internalization: Examining reasons for acting in two domains. *Journal of Personality and Social Psychology, 57,* 749–761.

Ryan, R. M., & Deci, E. L. (2000). Self-determination theory and the facilitation of intrinsic motivation, social development, and well-being. *American Psychologist, 55,* 68–78.

Salomon, G. (1983). The differential investment of mental effort in learning from different sources. *Educational Psychologist, 18,* 42–50.

Salomon, G. (1984). Television is "easy" and print is "tough:" The differential investment of mental effort in learning as a function of perceptions and attributions. *Journal of Educational Psychology, 76,* 647–658.

Salomon, G. (1987, September). *Beyond skill and knowledge: The role of mindfulness in learning and transfer.* Address to the Second European Conference for Research on Learning and Instruction, Tubingen, Germany.

Salomon, G., & Leigh, T. (1984). Predispositions about learning from print and television. *Journal of Communication, 20,* 119–135.

Sansone, C., & Harackiewicz, J. (1996). "I don't feel like it"; The function of self-interest in self-regulation. In L. Martin & A. Tesser (Eds.), *Striving and feeling: Interactions among goals, affect, and self-regulation* (pp. 203–228). Mahwah, NJ: Lawrence Erlbaum.

Scheidecker, D., & Freeman, W. (1998). *Bringing out the best in students: How legendary teachers motivate kids.* Thousand Oaks, CA: Corwin.

Schiefele, U. (1991). Interest, learning, and motivation. *Educational Psychologist, 26,* 299–323.

Schiefele, U., & Krapp, A. (1988, April). *The impact of interest on qualitative and structural indicators of knowledge.* Paper presented at the annual meeting of the American Educational Research Association, New Orleans, LA.

Schiefele, U., Krapp, A., & Winteler, A. (1988, April). *Conceptualization and mea-surement of interest.* Paper presented at the annual meeting of the American Educational Research Association, New Orleans, LA.

Schmeck, R. R. (Ed.). (1988). *Learning strategies and learning styles.* New York: Plenum.

Schmitt, A. P., & Crocker, L. (1981, April). *Improving performance on multiple choice tests.* Presentation at the annual meeting of the American Educational Research Association, Los Angeles, CA.

Schmoker, M. (2001). *The results fieldbook: Practical strategies from dramatically improved schools.* Alexandria, VA: Association for Supervision and Curriculum Development.

Schoenbach, R., Greenleaf, C., Cziko, C., & Hurwitz, L. (1999). *Reading for understanding: A guide to improving reading in middle and high school classrooms.* San Francisco: Jossey-Bass; WestEd.

Schön, D. A. (1987). *Educating the reflective practitioner: Toward a new design for teaching and learning in the professions.* San Francisco: Jossey-Bass.

Schroeder, C. C. (1993). New students—New learning styles. *Change, 25*(4), 21–26.

Schultheiss, D. P. (2000). Emotional-social issues in the provision of career counseling. In D. A. Luzzo (Ed.), *Career counseling of college students: An empirical guide to strategies that work* (pp. 43–62). Washington, DC: American Psychological Association.

Secretary's Commission on Achieving Necessary Skills (SCANS). (1991). *What work requires of schools: A SCANS report for America 2000.* Washington, DC: Author.

Seligman, M. (1990). *Learned optimism.* New York: Alfred A. Knopf.

Seligman, M. (1995). *The optimistic child.* Boston: Houghton Mifflin.

Senge, P. M. (1990). *The fifth discipline: The art and practice of the learning organization.* New York: Doubleday.

Senge, P. M., et al. (1994). *The fifth discipline fieldbook: Strategies and tools for building a learning organization.* New York: Currency, Doubleday.

Shanahan, T., and Neuman, S. (1997). Literacy research that makes a difference. *Reading Research Quarterly, 32*(2), 202–210.

Shapiro, L. (1997). *How to raise a child with a high EQ: A parent's guide to emotional intelligence.* New York: HarperCollins.

Sieber, J. E., O'Neil, H. F., Jr., & Tobias, S. (Eds.). (1977). Anxiety, learning, and instruction. Hillsdale, NJ: Lawrence Erlbaum.

Silberman, M. (1996). *Active learning: 101 strategies to teach any subject.* Boston: Allyn & Bacon.

Skinner, B. F. (1989). The origins of cognitive thought. *American Psychologist, 44,* 13–18.

Slavin, R. (2003). A reader's guide to scientifically based research. *Educational Leadership, 60*(5), 12–16.

Smith, C. P. (Ed.). (1992). *Motivation and personality: Handbook of thematic content analysis.* New York: Cambridge University Press.

Snow, R. E. (1977). Research on aptitude for learning: A progress report. In L. S. Shulman (Ed.), *Review of research in education, Vol. 4.* Itasca, IL: F. E. Peacock.

Snow, R. E. (1980). Aptitude processes. In R. E. Snow, P. A. Federico, & W. E. Montague (Eds.), *Aptitude learning and instruction, Vol. 1. Cognitive process analyses of aptitude* (pp. 27–64). Hillsdale, NJ: Lawrence Erlbaum.

Snow, R. E. (1989a). Cognitive-conative aptitude interactions in learning. In R. Kanfer, P. L. Ackerman, & R. Cudeck (Eds.), *Abilities, motivation, and methodology* (pp. 435–474). Hillsdale, NJ: Lawrence Erlbaum.

Snow, R. E. (1989b). Toward assessment of cognitive and conative structures in learning. *Educational Researcher, 118*(9), 8–14.

Snow, R. E. (1990). New approaches to cognitive and conative assessment in education. *International Journal of Educational Research, 14,* 455–473.

Snow, R. E. (1992). Aptitude theory: Yesterday, today, and tomorrow. *Educational Psychologist, 27,* 5–32.

Snow, R. E., Como, L., & Jackson III, D. N. (1996). Individual differences in affective and conative functions. In D. C. Berliner & R. C. Calfee (Eds.), *Handbook of educational psychology* (pp. 243–310). New York: Macmillan.

Snow, R. E., & Farr, M. J. (1987). Cognitive-conative-affective processes in aptitude, learning, and instruction: An introduction. In R. E. Snow & M. J. Farr (Eds.), *Aptitude, learning, and instruction: Vol. 3. Conative and affective process analyses* (pp. 1–8), Hillsdale, NJ: Lawrence Erlbaum.

Snow, R. E., & Jackson III, D. N. (1992). *Assessment of conative constructs for educational research and evaluation: A catalogue* (CSE Tech. Rep. No. 354). Los Angeles: University of California, National Center for Research on Evaluation, Standards, and Student Testing.

Solomon, R. (1980). The opponent-process theory of acquired motivation: The costs of pleasure and the benefits of pain. *American Psychologist, 8,* 691–712.

Spence, J.T., & Helmreich, R. L. (1983). Achievement related motives and behavior. In J. T. Spence (Ed.), *Achievement and achievement motives: Psychological and sociological approaches* (pp. 7–68). San Francisco: W. H. Freeman.

Stansberry, S.L., & Kymes, A.D. ((2007). Transforming learning through "Teaching With Technology" electronic portfolios. *Journal of Adolescent & Adult Literacy.*

Stein, N. L., & Oatley, K. (1992). Basic emotions: Theory and measurement. *Cognition and Emotion, 6,* 161–168.

Strelau, J. (1983). *Temperament, personality, activity.* New York: Academic.

Students say: What makes a good teacher? (1997). *Schools in the Middle, 6*(5), 15–17.

Strong, R., & Silver, H., Perini, M., & Tuculescu, G. (2003). Boredom and its opposite. *Educational Leadership, 61*(1). 24-29.

Sullo, B. (2007). *Activating the desire to learn.* Alexandria, VA.: Association for Supervision & Curriculum Development.

Sykes, G. (1996). Reform *of* and *as* professional development. *Phi Delta Kappan, 77*(7), 464–467.

Tallon, A. (1997). *Head and heart: Affection, cognition, volition as triune consciousness.* New York: Fordham University.

Tiberius, R. (1986). Metaphors underlying the improvement of teaching and learning. *British Journal of Educational Technology, 17*(2), 144–146.

Tomkins, S. S. (1984). Affect theory. In K. P. Scherer & P. Ekman (Eds.), *Approaches to emotion* (pp. 163–195). Hillsdale, NJ: Lawrence Erlbaum.

Urdan, T., & Maehr, M. (1995). Beyond a two-goal theory of motivation and achievement: A case for social goals. *Review of Educational Research, 65*(3), 213–243.

Vygotsky, I. (1978). Interaction between learning and development. In M. Cole, V. John-Steiner, S. Scribner, & E. Souberman. (Eds.), *Mind in society: The development of higher psychological process* (pp. 105–119). Cambridge, MA: Harvard University Press.

Wadsworth, W. C. (1995). *Once upon a time tales: How the sea became salt.* NY: Barnes & Noble, Inc.

Waitley, D. (1996). *The new dynamics of goal setting: Flextactics for a fast-changing world.* New York: William Morrow.

Walsh, W. B., & Betz, N. E. (1990). *Tests and assessment* (2nd ed.). Englewood Cliffs, NJ: Prentice Hall.

Warren, R. (1997). Engaging students in active learning. *About Campus, 2*(1),16–20.

Webster's Third New International Dictionary (Unabridged, 3rd ed.). (2002). Conation. Springfield, MA: Merriam-Webster.

Weiner, B. (1986). *An attribution theory of motivation and emotion.* New York: Springer-Verlag.

Weinstein, M. S. (1969). Achievement motivation and risk preference. *Journal of Personality and School Psychology, 13,* 153–172.

Wenger, E. (1998). *Communities of practice: Learning, meaning, and identity.* New York: Cambridge University Press.

Wenglinsky, H. (2002). How schools matter: The link between teacher classroom practices and student academic performance. *Education Policy Analysis Archives, 10*(12). Retrieved October 7, 2003 from http://epaa.asu.edu/epaa/v10n12/.

Wentzel, K. R. (1993). Motivation and achievement in early adolescence: The role of multiple classroom goals. *Journal of Early Adolescence, 13*(1), 4–20.

Wepner, S. B. (1991, October–November). The effects of a computerized reading program on "at-risk" secondary students. Paper presented at the annual meeting of the College Reading Association, Crystal City, VA. (ERIC Document Reproduction Service No. ED340006)

White, R. W. (1959). Motivation reconsidered: The concept of competence. *Psychological Review, 66,* 297–333.

Wiggins, J. S. (1979). A psychological taxonomy of trait-descriptive terms: The interpersonal domain. *Journal of Personality and Social Psychology, 37,* 395–412.

Williams, L. V. (1986). *Teaching for the two-sided mind: A guide to right brain/left brain education.* New York: Simon & Schuster.

Wilson, S. M., Peterson, P. L., Ball, L., & Cohen, D. K. (1996). Learning by all. *Phi Delta Kappan, 77*(7), 468–470, 472, 474–476.

Wiseman, D. G., & Hunt, G. H. (2001). *Best practice in motivation and management in the classroom.* Springfield, IL: C. C. Thomas.

Wohlsletter, P., & Briggs, K. L. (1994). The principal's role in school-based management. *Principal, 74*(2), 14, 16–17.

Wolfe, P. (2001). *Brain matters, Translating research into classroom practice.* Alexandria, VA: Association for Supervision and Curriculum Development.

Wood, K., D. (2006). Motivation, self-efficacy, and the engaged reader. *Middle School Journal, 37*(5), 55–59.

Woods, D. R. (1994). *Problem-based learning: How to gain the most from PBL.* Waterdown, Ontario, Canada: Donald R. Woods.

Woodward, W. R. (1982). The "discovery" of social behaviorism and social learning theory, 1870–1980. *American Psychologist, 37,* 396–410.

Ziglar, Z. (1994). *Over the top: Moving from survival to stability, from stability to success, from success to significance.* Nashville, TN: Thomas Nelson.

Zuroff, D. C., Moskowitz, D. S., & Coté, S. (1999). Dependency, self-criticism, interpersonal behaviour and affect: Evolutionary perspectives. *British Journal of Clinical Psychology, 38,* 231–250.

Index

CORWIN PRESS

The Corwin Press logo—a raven striding across an open book—represents the union of courage and learning. Corwin Press is committed to improving education for all learners by publishing books and other professional development resources for those serving the field of PreK–12 education. By providing practical, hands-on materials, Corwin Press continues to carry out the promise of its motto: **"Helping Educators Do Their Work Better."**